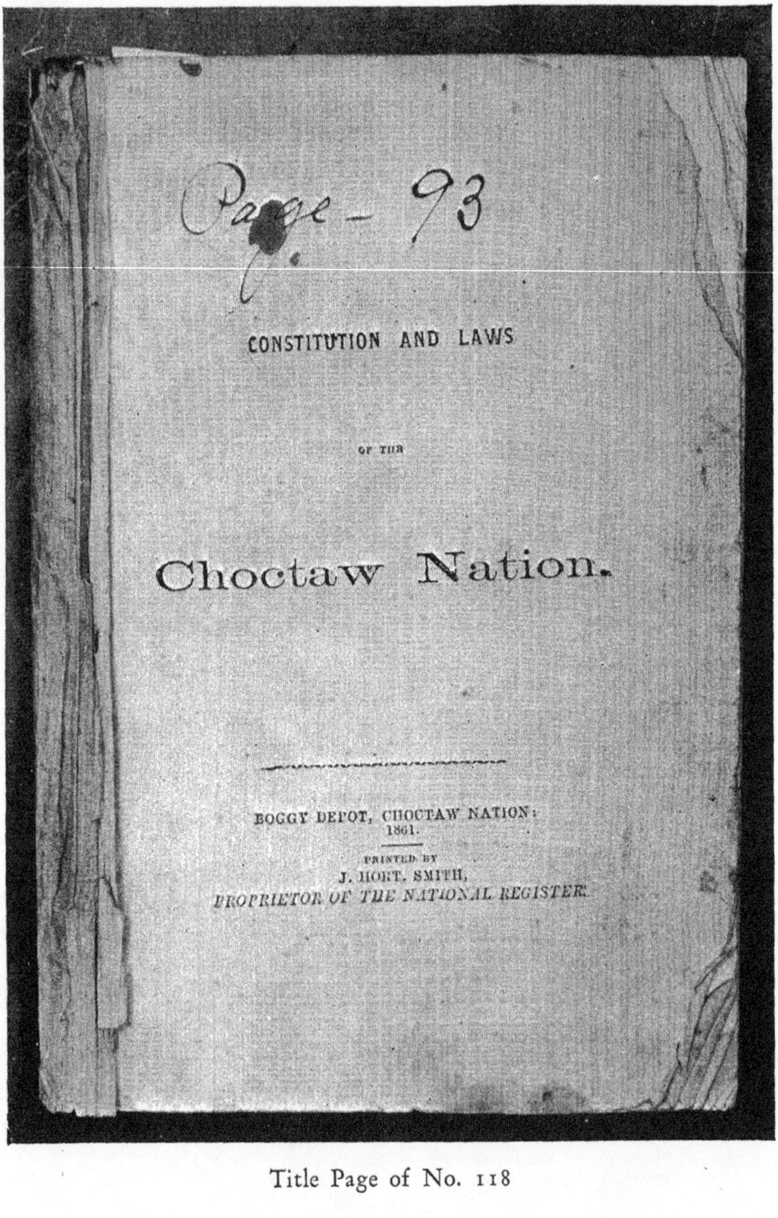


Title Page of No. 118

A BIBLIOGRAPHY OF

# THE CONSTITUTIONS AND LAWS OF THE AMERICAN INDIANS

BY

LESTER HARGRETT

WITH AN INTRODUCTION
BY JOHN R. SWANTON

THE LAWBOOK EXCHANGE, LTD.
Clark, New Jersey

ISBN 978-1-58477-260-6

Lawbook Exchange edition 2003, 2023

*The quality of this reprint is equivalent to the quality of the original work.*



**The Lawbook Exchange, Ltd.**
33 Terminal Avenue
Clark, New Jersey 07066-1321

*Please see our website for a selection of our other publications and fine facsimile reprints of classic works of legal history:*
www.lawbookexchange.com

**Library of Congress Cataloging-in-Publication Data**

Hargrett, Lester, 1902-1962.
A bibliography of the constitutions and laws of the American Indians / by Lester Hargrett ; with an introduction by John R. Swanton.
p. cm.
Originally published: Cambridge : Harvard University Press, 1947.
Includes bibliographical references and index.
ISBN 1-58477-260-3 (cloth: alk. paper)
1. Indians of North America—Legal status, laws, etc.—Bibliography. I. Title.

KF8220.A1 H3 2002
01 6.34273'02'08997—dc21 2002024313

*Printed in the United States of America on acid-free paper*

A BIBLIOGRAPHY OF

# THE CONSTITUTIONS AND LAWS OF THE AMERICAN INDIANS

BY

LESTER HARGRETT

WITH AN INTRODUCTION
BY JOHN R. SWANTON

CAMBRIDGE
HARVARD UNIVERSITY PRESS

1947

PRINTED IN THE UNITED STATES OF AMERICA

# PREFACE

This volume contains a descriptive list of the printed constitutions, and the statutes and session acts and resolutions passed by properly authorized bodies, of once semi-independent and self-governing Indian tribes and nations of the present United States, together with a few biographical and historical notes. Of the 225 publications described, well over one-third, many of them of the highest importance, have not hitherto been recorded in any connection, and the scant bibliographical information about the others is widely scattered and often imperfect.

Constitutional convention ordinances and resolutions and council rules have been included, as have a few volumes of Indian Territory local ordinances, but no effort has been made to exhaust these particular veins. The scattered occurrences of pertinent documents in newspapers and other periodicals and in federal and state publications have not been listed, since most of them appear anyway in volumes here described, nor have the numerous constitutions and charters which followed the Indian Reorganization Act and similar acts of Congress of 1934. Proposed acts, or bills, of which a number are known in printed copies, have not been included. Treaties do not fall within the province of this volume nor do federal or state laws on Indian affairs.

The great southern tribes, together with smaller neighbors whose development they influenced to some degree in later Indian Territory days, produced more than nine-tenths of the documents described in this volume. These documents have all lost their legal force, but they retain, in addition to incalculable historical value, the important record of an increasingly unified effort by a more or less concentrated group of Indian tribes to adjust themselves to changing conditions by means of self-government under constitutional forms observed to be successfully employed by the whites.

That these people were finally deprived of the autonomy guaranteed them by treaty was perhaps inevitable and it is now, like all injustice, of little concern except to the victims. It is more to the point that the experience which the Indian gained in constitutional self-government prepared him, when United States citizenship was thrust upon him, to live peaceably with his despoilers.

The growth of the movement mirrored in this volume is not readily apparent under the alphabetical arrangement by tribes adopted for convenience in the bibliography and a chronology of the principal events has been supplied in a preliminary table in order to remedy this defect. Sporadic efforts, like those recorded here of the northern and northwestern tribes, and others, although of some consequence, like those of the Seneca in New York, have been omitted from the chronology as being unrelated to the main movement which originated in the South and continued in Indian Territory after the removal thither of the large southern tribes.

A "talk" by President Jefferson to a Cherokee delegation visiting Washington City in 1809 so well illustrates the official encouragement early accorded Indian efforts to establish orderly self-government that its text has been included in an appendix. One might profitably read it first.

This volume is the outgrowth of notes first gathered to satisfy my own desire for a guide to an uncharted territory of American law and history and its preparation has been a private undertaking. My obligations to those who have so courteously aided me are therefore peculiarly personal and I wish here to renew my sincere thanks to all of them.

LESTER HARGRETT

Washington, D. C.
March 9, 1946.

# CONTENTS

# PLATES

# INTRODUCTION

This material, brought together so painstakingly by Mr. Hargrett, will add significantly to any library dealing with the history of the laws and political institutions of our country. It has interest both for the student of history and the student of law, and incidentally adds a chapter to the story of the development of printing in America. To the ethnologist who is concerned with problems of acculturation it will also be of great service, and although most questions bearing on the relations between our government and the Indian tribes are now settled, or in a fair way to being settled, our increasing involvement in world affairs and cumulative contacts with less advanced peoples will make these past experiences of ours of current value.

Upon the whole, the story told by this bibliography is what one familiar with Indian history might have expected. All the documents represent efforts by, or for, the tribes in question to adjust them to those new conditions brought about by European intrusion, and it is significant that more than nine-tenths of them are from the tribes most highly developed in pre-Columbian times and believed to have been mainly responsible for the construction of the great mounds. The only marked exception is the case of the Iroquois of New York who had anticipated the great crisis by forming the remarkable League of the Long House.

Events in the earlier history of North America which we may sense only obscurely had given Iroquoian peoples a training in organization which especially prepared them to meet the shock of a still more highly organized alien culture. But whereas in the north it was the admirable League that served in this emergency, in the case of the Cherokee it was rather the lack of a case-hardened national structure and their ability to adapt themselves to new situations. Both had, however, learned one lesson that many other tribes failed to grasp, the virtue of absorbing enemies rather than destroying them. Therefore, both grew steadily at the expense of related as well as non-related tribes. Both benefited, moreover, by the fact that they escaped the first shock of European contact and were even regarded by the early settlers as allies. The Cherokee enjoyed a further advantage in that they lived in the most rugged and easily defended mountain section of eastern North America, so that colonial settlements tended to flow round instead of over them thus giving them time for new adjustments. During this period they benefited from the absorption of remnants of other tribes driven inland. Like the Iroquois to the north and the Creeks, Choctaw, and Chickasaw to the south and west they became a nucleus of resistance to the invasion of the white man and the intrusion of his culture. They had an advantage over the tribes last mentioned, however, in their proximity to the initial English colonies of Virginia and South Carolina. Spanish Florida was older but failed to increase in numbers, nor did it protect effectively the tribes in its neighborhood which were consequently broken up by the better organized and better armed Creeks and by diseases, the remnants being forced to take refuge with stronger units.

And so it came about that, in the southeastern area, the problem of adaptation to a new civilization was taken up first by the Cherokee, and leadership ever afterwards remained in their hands. Invention of the Cherokee syllabary by Sequoya is a sufficient index of the effort of that tribe to solve this problem. How successfully they accomplished the adjustment is proved by their later history, by the fact that, instead of dying out, the Cherokee are today the most populous of all tribes within the limits of the present United States, and by the prominent men they have contributed to the life of our nation. Cherokee, or those claiming Cherokee affiliations, are today scattered everywhere. The leadership of this tribe in acculturation is reflected in the prominent part it took in efforts to found a united Indian state. And so it is not strange that, in the accompanying bibliography, Cherokee documents supply more than a third, actually about two-fifths, of the titles.

Second to Iroquoian peoples in adapting themselves to white

civilization—if we except the tribes of the northern hunting areas —were the Indians of the Muskhogean family who indeed formed four of the "Five Civilized Tribes." The largest numerically were the Choctaw. They showed a willingness even greater than that of the Cherokee to respond to altered conditions, but were nearly half a century behind the Cherokee in the call to face this new emergency. Not until the French settled Louisiana in 1699 was the problem presented to them, and their development was still further delayed by wars between the French and English and their own incidental struggles with their cousins the Chickasaw. Nevertheless, they adapted themselves more rapidly than any other southern tribe except the Cherokee, as is faithfully indicated by the number of Choctaw titles in the present bibliography, of which they constitute about one-fourth.

The Creek Indians, represented by about one-eighth of the titles, although fewer in numbers than the Choctaw, dispute with them the leadership among Muskhogean peoples, owing to a national organization of pre-Columbian origin comparable in many ways to that of the Iroquois, their high cultural development, their warlike prowess, and the very important part they played in the history of our country. They were held back, however, in effecting an adjustment to white culture, by the tenacity of their own highly developed social and religious organization, and by the fact that they were forced to defend themselves for nearly a century against the machinations and aggressions of the three most powerful European nations, England, France, and Spain. Nevertheless, Creek titles stand third in number. On historical grounds this tribe, or rather Confederation, should be rated second, and, indeed, first on the ground of their pre-Columbian attainments in government.

The Chickasaw have always been numerically inferior to the three tribes already considered, but were as famous in the south for their warlike prowess as the Iroquois in the north, and like the Iroquois they constituted the forefront of British power and were responsible in large measure for the failure of French colonial ambitions. The fact that their language is almost identical with that of the

Choctaw and the further fact that they constituted for a time part of the Choctaw Nation in Indian Territory, naturally tended to limit the number of strictly Chickasaw documents, so that twenty titles make a very respectable showing.

To one familiar with Seminole history the fact that they are represented by but a single document is not surprising, for they were made up of the extreme conservatives of the Creek Nation who emigrated to Florida largely to escape the discipline and acculturation to which the Creeks proper were exposed and maintained, as we know, one of the longest and bloodiest wars in the entire history of our relations with the Indians.

Of the tribes responsible for the remaining documents in Mr. Hargrett's collection we note that two, the Osage and the allied Sauk and Fox, were living, at the time when their constitutions and laws were printed, in the immediate neighborhood of those already considered which may have furnished the stimulus for such action. The same may also have been the case with the Ottawa band in Kansas. Since the Osage and Omaha Indians are closely related and the code of one was printed within a year of the constitution of the other, it may be suspected that stimulus was at work here. It may be assumed plausibly as well in the case of the Winnebago, who lived near the Omaha, since their laws and regulations were committed to print only eight years after those of the latter tribe.

For the Six Nations as a whole, the ancient Long House organization seems to have sufficed. From time to time, however, there were independence movements in the separate tribes, and it is not singular that the strongest should have been among the Seneca, for this tribe was the last taken into the Confederation, maintained more independence of action than the rest, and had also annexed several formerly independent peoples. It would also seem that the movement represented by the documents in this collection was stimulated in some measure by the Hicksite Friends. We probably owe the Stockbridge and Munsee document to the long acquaintance of those tribes with the whites of New England and New York. The Nez Percé code stands by itself and seems to have been a product of white promotion rather than of spontaneous Indian origination.

As outreachings toward adjustment with the era ushered in by white intrusion all of these documents are interesting and seem to reflect accurately the strength of such movements in different sections of the country. With most tribes the effort was ephemeral and they either succumbed completely or continued their native institutions as well as they could down to the inevitable end, but among our southern Indians there was a long and well marked transition period during which they slowly qualified for citizenship in the American nation by maintenance of local governments intermediate between their ancient forms and those prevalent among the whites. This intermediate period is clearly and forcibly reflected in the documents of Mr. Hargrett's collection. The extent to which the experiments of the Indians of the Five Civilized Tribes prepared them for wider collective thinking is illustrated by their efforts to set up a union government for the tribes of Indian Territory in 1870–1875, their later efforts in 1905 in favor of the all-Indian State of Sequoyah, and finally in the number of eminent men they have contributed to our national life.

JOHN R. SWANTON

March 22, 1946.

# CHRONOLOGY OF PRINCIPAL EVENTS

1736 Christian Priber tries to organize a national Cherokee government.

1799 William Augustus Bowles sets up among the Lower Creeks the artificial and short-lived State of Muskogee.
Benjamin Hawkins, a United States Indian agent, persuades the Upper Creeks to inaugurate an elementary national government.

1808 The Cherokee begin to write their laws.

1817 The Creeks begin to write their laws.

1820 The Western (or Arkansas) Cherokee orally adopt their first law.

1821 The Cherokee Nation begins the regular printing of its laws.

1824 The Western (or Arkansas) Cherokee begin to write their laws.

1825 Seminole chiefs in Florida subscribe to a written law.

1826 The Choctaw in Mississippi adopt a constitution.
The Creeks adopt a code of laws.

1827 The Cherokee Nation adopts a constitution.

1828 Georgia nullifies Indian autonomy within its borders.

1830 Mississippi nullifies Indian autonomy within its borders.

1834 The Choctaw reëstablish national government in the West and adopt a new constitution.

1839 The reunited Cherokee establish national government in the West and adopt their permanent constitution.

1840 The Choctaw Nation begins the regular printing of its laws.

1841 The Creeks reëstablish their government in the West.

1844 The Chickasaw tribe, forming at the time a district of the Choctaw Nation, begins to write its laws.

1846 The Chickasaw tribe adopts a constitution.

1849 The Chickasaw tribe first prints one of its laws.

1856 The Seminole Nation is organized in the West and a written constitution adopted shortly afterward.

1857 The Chickasaw, now separated by treaty from the Choctaw, organize the Chickasaw Nation, adopt a constitution, and begin the regular printing of their laws.

1859 The Creek Nation adopts a constitution.

1860 The Choctaw Nation adopts its permanent constitution.

1861 The Osage Nation in Kansas adopts a constitution.

1867 The Creek Nation adopts its permanent constitution.
The Chickasaw Nation adopts its permanent constitution.

1868 The Creek Nation begins to print its laws.

1870 The General Council of the Indian Territory writes a constitution, never ratified, for a proposed Indian Territory.

1881 The Osage Nation in Indian Territory adopts its permanent constitution.

1885 The Sac and Fox Nation in Indian Territory adopts a constitution.

1905 The constitution of the proposed all-Indian State of Sequoyah is adopted in a convention of the people of Indian Territory and ratified at a general election.

1906 Tribal governments in Indian Territory are abolished by Congress and their subjects made citizens of the United States.

# EXPLANATION AND KEY TO LOCATION SYMBOLS

All texts are in the English language unless otherwise described. Entries are arranged chronologically by date of printing under the appropriate tribe in its alphabetical order. Size is expressed by height, in nearest half centimeters, of the largest copy seen. A single leaf printed on one side only is described as a broadside; one printed on both sides, as a broadsheet. Of those entries for which no locations are given it is to be understood that ten or more copies have been seen or reliably reported and that the volume is to be found in the principal law libraries and in the library of the Thomas Gilcrease Foundation at Tulsa, Oklahoma. Locations of incomplete copies have not been noted except in rare instances where the only known copy of a volume is itself incomplete.

| | |
|---|---|
| **C** | California State Library, Sacramento, California. |
| **CSmH** | Henry E. Huntington Library and Art Gallery, San Marino, California. |
| **CSt** | Stanford University Libraries, Stanford University, California. |
| **CU-Law** | University of California Law School Library, Berkeley, California. |
| **CtY** | Yale University Library, New Haven, Connecticut. |
| **CtY-L** | Yale Law School Library, New Haven, Connecticut. |
| **DIA** | U. S. Office of Indian Affairs Library, Washington, D. C.[1] |
| **DIA-S** | U. S. Office of Indian Affairs, Office of the Solicitor, Washington, D. C.[1] |
| **DJ** | U. S. Department of Justice Library, Washington, D. C. |
| **DLC** | Library of Congress, Washington, D. C. |
| **DNA** | National Archives, Washington, D. C. |

[1] Temporarily at Chicago, Illinois.

| | |
|---|---|
| DSI-E | Bureau of American Ethnology Library, Smithsonian Institution, Washington, D. C. |
| ICLaw | Chicago Law Institute, Chicago, Illinois. |
| ICN | Newberry Library, Chicago, Illinois. |
| In-SC | Indiana Supreme Court Library, Indianapolis, Indiana. |
| Ia-L | Iowa State Law Library, Des Moines, Iowa. |
| IaU-L | State University of Iowa Law Library, Iowa City, Iowa. |
| KHi | Kansas State Historical Society, Topeka, Kansas. |
| M | Massachusetts State Library, Boston, Massachusetts. |
| MB | Boston Public Library, Boston, Massachusetts. |
| MBAt | Library of the Boston Athenaeum, Boston, Massachusetts. |
| MH | Harvard College Library, Cambridge, Massachusetts. |
| MH-L | Harvard University Law School Library, Cambridge, Massachusetts.[2] |
| MWA | American Antiquarian Society, Worcester, Massachusetts. |
| MiU-L | University of Michigan Law Library, Ann Arbor, Michigan. |
| MnHi | Minnesota Historical Society, St. Paul, Minnesota. |
| MnU-L | University of Minnesota Law School Library, Minneapolis, Minnesota. |
| MoS | St. Louis Public Library, St. Louis, Missouri. |
| MoSL | Law Library Association of St. Louis, St. Louis, Missouri. |
| MoU | University of Missouri Library, Columbia, Missouri. |
| N-L | New York State Law Library, Albany, New York. |
| NHi | New York Historical Society, New York City. |
| NN | New York Public Library, New York City. |
| NNB | Association of the Bar of the City of New York, New York City. |
| NNLI | New York Law Institute, New York City. |
| Ok | Oklahoma State Library, Oklahoma City, Oklahoma. |
| OkHi | Oklahoma Historical Society, Oklahoma City, Oklahoma. |

[2] A list of this library's splendid collection of Indian laws, with a few titles from other sources, will be found in the *Law Library Journal,* XXXIV (1941), 126–148. It was compiled by Mr. Robert B. Anderson, at the time assistant librarian.

| | |
|---|---|
| OkMu | Muskogee Public Library, Muskogee, Oklahoma. |
| OkTG | Library of the Thomas Gilcrease Foundation, Tulsa, Oklahoma. |
| OkTahT | Northeastern State Teachers' College Library, Tahlequah, Oklahoma. |
| OkU | University of Oklahoma Library, Norman, Oklahoma. |
| OkU-P | University of Oklahoma Library, Frank Phillips Collection, Norman, Oklahoma. |
| PHi | Historical Society of Pennsylvania, Philadelphia, Pennsylvania. |
| PPB | Philadelphia Bar Association, Philadelphia, Pennsylvania. |
| T | Tennessee State Library, Nashville, Tennessee. |
| TxU | University of Texas Library, Austin, Texas. |
| WHi | State Historical Society of Wisconsin, Madison, Wisconsin. |

| | |
|---|---|
| Graff | Mr. Everett D. Graff, Winnetka, Illinois. |
| Shleppey | Mr. John W. Shleppey, Tulsa, Oklahoma. |
| Streeter | Mr. Thomas W. Streeter, Morristown, New Jersey. |
| Wright | Miss Muriel H. Wright, Oklahoma City, Oklahoma. |

A BIBLIOGRAPHY OF

# THE CONSTITUTIONS AND LAWS OF THE AMERICAN INDIANS

# THE CHEROKEE NATION

The Cherokee Indians, an Iroquoian tribe, once held a large part of the southeastern United States, where they were first observed in 1540 by Hernando de Soto and where subsequent travelers found them scattered over 80 or more loosely allied towns and villages. By the nineteenth century, treaties and wars had reduced their holdings to a comparatively small area in the southern Appalachians. Stimulated by the infused blood of energetic white traders and soldiers, raised to literacy almost overnight by the introduction of a syllabary of their language devised by one of their own number, and for many years a special object of Protestant missionary concern, the Cherokee had begun to make rapid progress in civilization when the advance of white settlers forced the removal, completed in 1839, of the main body of them to Indian Territory. There they absorbed the Western (or Arkansas) Cherokee, afterwards known as Old Settlers, a vanguard of their number who had removed from the East about twenty years earlier and who already had a government of their own with written laws.[1] After long and bitter civil strife and a ruinous alliance with the Confederate States of America the Cherokee settled down to a life of agriculture and trade. Comprising the largest group of the so-called Five Civilized Tribes, they became citizens of the United States in 1906 when their own government came to an end. The greatest of several first-rate men produced by the tribe were George Guess or Sequoya (1770?–1843) and John Ross or Guwisguwi (1790–1866).

Probably the earliest effort to introduce European notions of government among the Cherokee—and indeed among the Indians of the present United States—was made in 1736 by Christian Gottlieb Priber, or Pierre Albert, as one early narrator knew him,

[1] See No. 18 of this bibliography.

a German or Swiss adventurer who yearned to put into practice some of the revolutionary social doctrines then stirring in France. Priber planned a communistic Cherokee republic but his scheme died with him.[2]

The earliest known written law of the Cherokee Indians is one adopted September 11, 1808, "by the Chiefs and Warriors in a National Council assembled" at Brooms Town in the Cherokee Nation in Georgia.[3] It is printed in No. 1 of this bibliography.

The 1827 constitution, which was modeled closely upon that of the United States, and again the 1839 constitution, which, with few changes, remained in force until dissolution of the Cherokee government in 1906, vested legislative authority in a bicameral council which met annually and whose members were elected by the people, executive authority in a principal chief similarly chosen, and judicial authority in a supreme court whose members were elected by the council.

When the main body of the tribe was pitchforked to the West a few hundred of the Cherokee fled to the mountains of western North Carolina where their descendants, now numbering about 2000, live on a reservation given to them by the state. They have long been citizens of North Carolina and for over a century have maintained no tribal connection with the Cherokee in the West.

Most of the translations of Cherokee names in the following pages rest upon the authority of Mr. Richard R. Glory (Uleyuñha), a full blood Cherokee, of Stilwell, Oklahoma, Mr. Levi B. Gritts (Newaduñ), almost a full blood, of Muskogee, Oklahoma, and Mr. Will West Long (Ganuñhida), almost a full blood, of the village of Big Cove in the Eastern Cherokee Reservation in

[2] Upon joining the Cherokee, Priber laid aside European habit, quickly mastered the difficult native tongue, and attached himself to "Emperor" Moytoy, one of the strongest chiefs of the tribe, as His Majesty's Principal Secretary of State, a title under which he addressed startling diplomatic communications to neighboring colonial governors. He greatly strengthened his influence over the Indians by thinking up magnificent and resounding titles for Moytoy to bestow upon his fellow chiefs. A sharp thorn to the English, Priber was taken by a party of Carolina traders and Creek Indians and cast into prison at Frederica in Georgia where he died in 1741.

[3] It is interesting to note that this law antedated by four months President Jefferson's talk to the Deputies of the Cherokee Upper Towns quoted in the Appendix.

North Carolina; a few are from James Mooney, *Myths of the Cherokee* (1902).

**Laws of the Cherokee Nation,** passed by the National Committee and Council. Printed by order of the Committee and Council. Knoxville, printed at the Knoxville Register Office by Heiskell & Brown, 1821. [1

23 p. 19 cm.

One act each of the sessions of September 1808, April 1810, and May 1817, and acts and resolutions of the regular October sessions of 1819 and 1820.

This volume, printed at Knoxville, Tennessee, is the earliest known publication of the laws of an American Indian government. Heiskell & Brown had printed in 1819 a Cherokee spelling-book in the Roman alphabet, the first book in the language.

NHi NN

**Laws of the Cherokee Nation;** adopted by the Council at various periods. Printed for the benefit of the Nation. "Knoxville Register" Office; printed by Heiskell & Brown, Knoxville, T. 1826. [2

75 p., 9 unnumbered leaves, a census table on the recto of each. 20 cm.

The contents of the preceding volume, acts and resolutions of the regular October sessions annually from 1821 to 1825, inclusive, one act of the extra session of June 1825, the Cherokee-Creek treaties of 1822 and 1823, and a census by districts of the Cherokee Nation.

NNB NNLI WHi

**Constitution of the Cherokee Nation,** made and established at a general convention of delegates, duly authorised for that purpose, at New Echota, July 26, 1827. Printed for the Cherokee Nation, at the Office of the Statesman and Patriot, Georgia. [Milledgeville, 1827.] [3

16 p. 18 cm. Errata slip inserted after title.

The president of the convention was John Ross or Guwisguwi[4] (1790–

[4] Guwisguwi, as has often been explained, is the Cherokee word for an unidentified large white bird of rare occurrence in the South. In his childhood Ross was called Tsanusdi, that is, Little John. In official literature printed in the Cherokee language his name often appears as Tsani (that is, John) Guwisguwi.

1866), a Cherokee mixed blood of Scottish descent, a statesman of extraordinary skill, and one of the great men of the Indian race. Ross was elected principal chief of the Cherokee Nation in the East in 1828 and served as such until the gathering of his people in the West in 1838 when he was elected principal chief of the reunited nation. This office he held until his death although for most of the Civil War period his right to it was contested by the southern faction of the tribe and for some months after the war disputed by the United States government.

New Echota, sometimes called New Town, was the capital town of the Cherokee Nation for several years before the removal of the tribe. It lay at the junction of the Oostanaula and Conasauga rivers in the present Gordon County, Georgia.

DLC MH-L NHi NN

Constitution of the Cherokee Nation, formed by a convention of delegates from the several districts, at New Echota, July 1827. [New Echota, 1828.] [4

28 p. 19.5 cm. Caption title. English and Cherokee versions in parallel columns.

The volume was printed on the pioneer American Indian press at New Echota in 1828; probably the first production after a few issues of the national newspaper, the *Cherokee Phoenix,* it was also the first book to make use of the Sequoyan syllabary. The printers were two white men, Isaac H. Harris and John F. Wheeler. The translation into Cherokee was made by the mixed blood Elias Boudinot.

Elias Boudinot or Galagina[5] (1802–1839) was one of the ablest men of the tribe, and his people's progress in civilization was sharply quickened by his zeal and energy. On a lecture tour of the East in 1826 he raised most of the money for a printing press for the Cherokee and he served as the first editor of the *Phoenix.* The missionary Worcester leaned heavily upon him in their joint translations of gospels, hymns, and tracts, and indeed from 1827 until his death there was hardly a publication in the Cherokee language in which he did not have a large hand. Boudinot was butchered

[5] That is, male deer or buck. The son of Uwâti, who was known to the whites as Christian David Watie, young Boudinot was called Buck Watie until he entered a missionary school at Cornwall, Connecticut, and took the name of the Philadelphia friend of Indian education. His brothers, one of them Stand Watie or Degatâga, the Confederate brigadier general, kept for a surname among the whites the abbreviation of Uwâti, their father's Indian name.

in the West in 1839 for signing the New Echota treaty of 1835 which committed the Cherokee to removal.

Isaac Heylin Harris, a native of Jasper, Tennessee, was appointed principal printer for the Cherokee Nation by the national council in October 1826 and authorized to engage an assistant printer. John Fisher Wheeler (1808–1880), a native of Kentucky, who had worked with Harris for the printer Dandridge Ferness at Huntsville, Alabama, agreed to join him, and together, with but one horse between them, they traveled from Jasper to New Echota in December 1827. John Walker Candy (1806?–1868), a young half blood Cherokee, was signed as apprentice, as later were two other Cherokee youths, Thomas Black Watie, a younger brother of the editor, and Mark Tyger or Damaga,[6] who seems to have been a younger brother of the prominent Dirt Thrower Tyger. Printing press and type arrived in January from Boston where the Cherokee font had been cast under the eye of Samuel Austin Worcester (1798–1859), a Presbyterian missionary to the Cherokee and the main hand in the enterprise,[7] and printing was begun in February 1828 on paper for which Harris had made a two weeks' wagon journey to Knoxville, Tennessee. The equipment, largely the gift of popular subscription, was the property of the Cherokee Nation, and the establishment was directed by Elias Boudinot, whose post of editor of the national newspaper was an office of the government.

A Methodist of telltale sectarian zeal, Harris grew militant in 1830 and noisily threatened to kick all his unregenerate superiors, the principal chief himself included. He was dismissed at the end of the year and forcibly removed from the nation, and Wheeler, now married to a sister of the native editor,[8] succeeded to the office of national printer. Wheeler's own

[6] That is, horsefly.

[7] A life long pagan, like many a conservative Cherokee, Sequoya is reputed to have said that he would never have devised his syllabary had he foreseen that it would be taken over by Christian missionaries.

[8] The superior Cherokee, Chickasaw, and Choctaw were increasingly exempt from the white taboo against intermarriage with people of color. Possessing no highly organized social or religious systems of their own to be doggedly preserved, they accepted new ways more easily than most of their red brothers and growing numbers of them embraced the Christian faith and eagerly sent their children to mission schools. With the steady approach of white people bringing negro slaves and with the attendant rise of a slaveholding class of their own, the southern Indians (the Creeks and their Seminole cousins excepted) developed a corollary taboo of their own against intermarriage with black inferiors, a prohibition conducive to good personal relations with well-disposed white neighbors and with missionaries, government agents, and others by choice or necessity sojourning among them. Loyal, patient, and hospitable, the southern Indians possessed native dignity of a high order and some of them, notably the Chickasaw, had

name was prudently dropped from the masthead of the *Phoenix* in April 1831 and replaced by that of John Candy, his three years' apprenticeship served and himself now married to another sister of the editor, when the State of Georgia, having thrust its laws over the Indian country within its chartered limits, moved to put down missionaries and other white men among the Cherokee known to dispute state sovereignty and suspected of encouraging Cherokee resistance. Wheeler stayed at his post, however, and in September he and ten others were seized by the Georgia Guard [9] for continuing in the Cherokee country without license and were tried and convicted and sentenced to four years at hard labor in the state penitentiary at Milledgeville. One of nine humanely pardoned by the governor when they recanted at the prison door and swore allegiance to the state, Wheeler secured the mandatory license and returned to the printing office at New Echota and to his part-time trade there in skins and furs.

The defiant Worcester mending shoes in prison, the editor Boudinot forced out of office in 1832 by deep division within the tribe, Georgia officers and squatters now in full cry, and many Cherokee smoked out and retreating to the West, the volume of printing at New Echota steadily shrank. Wheeler left for Indian Territory early in 1834 and the *Phoenix*, issued for some time with growing infrequency, last appeared in May of that year. The printing press was seized in October 1835 by Georgia officers and the following year Principal Chief John Ross complained to

---

marked agreeableness of person. In short, they were an eminently decent people and in consequence there is in Oklahoma with its large Indian minority no white prejudice today against Indian blood.

[9] A county militia positively fearless in times of peace in defending the borders of the state by rendering the fine Indian country beyond those borders troubled and unsafe for its ancient proprietors and their friends. A sample of the savage mischiefs which lay in store for captives of this band of whiteskins may be found in a sprightly narrative by John Howard Payne which appeared in December 1835 in the *Knoxville* (Tennessee) *Register* and which was reprinted the next month, with strangely false editorial groans, by the *North American Quarterly Magazine* (Philadelphia) for frost-bitten easterners covertly envious of the rip-snorting fire-eaters of the South and consequently hungry for the latest fearful revelations from that hot-blooded region. Seized by the Georgia Guard, which had invaded the sovereign State of Tennessee for the purpose, and accused of plotting with cutthroat French Jesuits and with scalp-crazed Principal Chief John Ross a joint Indian and negro uprising for the universal massacre of white Protestants, Payne was loghoused for twelve days and nights of blows, curses, and slops and then kicked out of Georgia. With noteworthy restraint and even with professional appreciation, in safe retrospect, of the extravagant humors of some of the clowns in the farce, Payne drew an irreverent picture of the Georgia Guard truthful enough to be regarded ever since by hypersensitive Georgia patriots as evidence that the scoundrel all along deserved not only jailing but probably hanging as well.

the Secretary of War that agents of the United States were using it in Tennessee to print attacks upon Cherokee leaders opposed to removal of the tribe.

MBAt MWA Streeter

Laws of the Cherokee Nation, enacted by the General Council in 1826, 1827 & 1828. Printed for the Cherokee Nation. Office of the "Cherokee Phoenix"; printed by Isaac Heylin Harris, New Echota, C. N. 1828. [5

45 p. 24 cm.

Acts and resolutions of the regular October sessions of 1826, 1827, and 1828, and one act of the extra session of July 1827.

MBAt NN NNLI WHi Streeter

Laws of the Cherokee Nation, enacted by the General Council in the year 1829. Printed for the Cherokee Nation. New Echota, Cherokee Nation. Office of the "Cherokee Phoenix." John F. Wheeler, printer. 1830. [6

18 p. 21 cm.

Acts and resolutions of the regular session of October 1829.

John F. Wheeler left New Echota in 1834 and joined the growing number of Cherokee in the West. Engaged by the missionary Worcester, lately freed from prison in Georgia, to run the press set up in August 1835 at the old Union Mission on the Grand River, five miles northeast of the present village of Mazie, in Mayes County, Wheeler was the first printer to work at his trade in present Oklahoma. After mission and press were removed to Park Hill in 1837 he served as printer there. Closely connected by marriage with the leaders of the minority faction of the Cherokee, Wheeler departed in haste after their bloody slaughter in 1839 and prudently stayed away in the troubled years that immediately followed. In early 1843 he was joint editor and proprietor with Thomas Sterne of the *Arkansas Intelligencer* at Van Buren, Arkansas, but in 1844, 1845, and 1846 he was back at Park Hill, where he and John Candy together printed several small volumes.

In 1847 Wheeler established a newspaper, the first, at Fort Smith, Arkansas, where publishing enterprises engaged him until his death there in 1880. He served at various times as city court judge, mayor of Fort Smith, and state senator. His Fort Smith imprint will be found on Chickasaw and

Choctaw volumes described further on in this bibliography. Judge Wheeler was born near Danville, Kentucky, in 1808.

MBAt NN NNLI WHi Streeter

An act passed by the Georgia legislature in 1828 outlawed the Cherokee government in that state after June 1, 1830. While John Ross continued to act as principal chief of the tribe and was tacitly recognized as such by Georgia authorities, the normal functions of government were suspended. No elections were held after 1830 and the council met only infrequently, and then just across the Georgia line, in Tennessee. Tribal government was not restored until the Cherokee were reunited in the West in 1839.

The constitution and laws of the Cherokee Nation: passed at Tah-le-quah, Cherokee Nation, 1839. Washington: printed by Gales and Seaton. 1840. [7

36 p. 19.5 cm. Printed wrappers.

The act of union between the Eastern and Western Cherokee adopted in convention July 12, 1839, at Illinois Camp Ground, two and a half miles southeast of Tahlequah, the constitution adopted in convention at Tahlequah[10] September 6, 1839, and acts and resolutions of the regular session of September 1839.

The constitution was largely drafted by the mixed blood William Shorey Coodey or Dâyunita[11] (1806–1849), a nephew of Principal Chief John Ross and his able assistant in many important capacities. The quality of his work may be measured by the fact that this instrument, with few amendments, met the needs of the Cherokee for the remainder of their tribal life. In an interview in 1840 with the astonished Secretary of War, Coodey stoutly defended the Cherokee political murders a year earlier. The expression of such a view, even when it was most strongly held, was customarily reserved for the deathbed or the barroom.

There were two presidents of the convention which adopted the act of union—the famous George Guess or Sequoya[12] (1770?–1843) for the Western Cherokee and the venerable George Lowrey or Agili[13] (1770?–

[10] Tahlequah was made the permanent capital of the Cherokee nation in 1839. The town was incorporated by the national council in 1852.

[11] That is, young beaver.

[12] Sequoya and Sequoyah are the popular spellings. Siquâyi would perhaps more nearly approximate the Cherokee. The meaning of the name has been lost.

[13] Agili is thought to be a contraction of Aginagili, the name of an eighteenth century chief and a Cherokee word which means rising fawn. Major Lowrey's name is often found in Cherokee literature as Tsatsi (that is, George) Agili.

1852) for the newly arrived Eastern Cherokee. Major Lowrey, a cousin of Sequoya and one of the first to encourage the great inventor, was president of the subsequent convention which adopted the constitution. He was for many years assistant principal chief and the official notice in the *Advocate* of his death stated that he had been "for over 60 years actively engaged in aiding and directing the affairs of the Nation." A temperance tract from his hand, first issued at Park Hill in 1842, is one of the earliest original native compositions printed in the Cherokee language.

The Gales and Seaton edition of the constitution and 1839 acts and resolutions is the earliest of several volumes of Indian laws printed at Washington over a long period and described in this bibliography. Not United States public documents, which have been excluded from this list, they were executed by private printing firms at the order usually of tribal delegates visiting Washington on official business.

## Resolutions. [Park Hill, 1841.] [8

Broadside. 30.5 cm. 2 columns. Text in English and in Cherokee.

The resolutions, dated "near Tahliquah, Jan. 16th, 1841," and signed by fifteen leading men of the dominant political party, here styled "Members of the Committee in behalf of the people," set up an extra-legal police force and court to forestall a reported factional plot against the lives of Principal Chief John Ross, Chief Justice Jesse Bushyhead, and other high public officials. The resolutions provided for this machinery of popular law to continue in operation "until laws to counteract such disorders may be passed by the people's national legislature."

The leaf was printed by John Candy on the mission press at Park Hill, the residence of Principal Chief John Ross and the center of Presbyterian missionary, educational, and printing activities. Park Hill, a village about four miles southwest of Tahlequah, was the second place of printing in present Oklahoma. The press continued in operation there until 1860 when the imminence of war put an end to northern missionary activities.

The mixed blood John Walker Candy has already been noticed as an apprentice and later a full fledged printer at the *Phoenix* office at New Echota in Georgia. He reached Indian Territory in late 1835 and was soon employed by Worcester as a translator and printer at the Union Mission press. After removal of mission and press to Park Hill, he worked there until 1847, printing, among other things, the earliest volume of Choctaw laws, in 1840. Candy was not too busy to serve in 1839 as clerk of the national council of the Western Cherokee. In 1852 he was engaged with others at the *Advocate* office at Tahlequah in printing the compiled laws of the Cherokee Nation and in December of that year he was elected, along with his fellow printer, Mark Tyger, himself a former New Echota apprentice, to Tahlequah's first town council. Candy was the printer at the Baptist Mission press at Cherokee in 1855. After the death of his first wife, who was a sister of Elias Boudinot and Stand Watie, he married a woman of the Stockbridge tribe, the widow of a Mohawk Indian who was a Methodist missionary to the Seneca. Candy was born in Georgia about 1806 and died, right after walking eight miles to church and back, near Webbers Falls, Cherokee Nation, in 1868. John F. Wheeler, who had known him well for forty years, wrote of Jack Candy that he was "an honest, upright good man in all his dealings with his fellow man." [14]

OkU-P

The constitution and laws of the Cherokee Nation: passed at Tah-le-quah, Cherokee Nation, 1839, 1840. Translated into the Cherokee language. Park Hill. Mission press: John Candy, printer, 1842. [9

52, [2] p. 17 cm. Joint English and Cherokee title. Text in Cherokee, with captions in English and Cherokee.

Act of union, constitution, and acts and resolutions of September 1839 and November 1840.

1000 copies were printed.

The translation was probably the work of the mixed blood Stephen Foreman or Utseluñnuñhi[15] (1807–1881), a well-known Cherokee school teacher and Presbyterian preacher. Educated at the College of New Jersey (now Princeton University) and formerly interpreter for the missionaries at Brainerd Mission in Tennessee and associate editor of the *Cherokee Phoenix* at New Echota in Georgia, Foreman became Worcester's top hand, after the assassination in 1839 of Elias Boudinot, in translating into Cherokee a long stream of tracts and Bible portions. He was elected to the

[14] Candy's Cherokee name was Dâguwadâ, a word which means redbird. Another former New Echota apprentice, Thomas Black Watie, a younger brother of Elias Boudinot and Stand Watie and John Candy's brother-in-law, worked for a time at the Park Hill printing office in its early years. Busy in the reprisals which darkened Cherokee soil after the assassinations of 1839, Tom Watie killed three of his enemies before he was himself shot down in November 1845. John Mix Stanley, who painted his portrait at Tahlequah in 1842, described him as "a fine-looking man, but abandoned and dissipated."

[15] That is, masquerader or pretender. The name is an old one in the tribe.

Cherokee supreme court in 1844 and was an executive councillor from 1847 to 1855.

**Streeter**

Laws of the Cherokee Nation, enacted by the National Council at their annual session A. D. 1841. Park Hill: Mission press: John Candy, printer. 1842. [10

24 p. 17 cm.

Acts and resolutions of the regular session of October 1841.

**Streeter**

The laws of the Cherokee Nation: passed at Tah-le-quah, Cherokee Nation, 1840, '41, '42, & '43. Cherokee: Baptist Mission press. H. Upham, printer. 1844. [11

72 p. 18 cm.

Acts and resolutions of the regular session of November 1840, October 1841, November 1842, and October 1843.

The Baptist Mission press was located at Cherokee,[16] known also as Bread Town, as Baptist, and as Bushyheadville, a village in the Going Snake District of the Cherokee Nation four miles north of the present Westville, Oklahoma, and three miles west of the Arkansas line. Established in 1843 by the Reverend Evan Jones,[17] a missionary who had commanded a detachment of emigrants in the removal, it was the second press operated in present Oklahoma although its location was the third place of printing, the press established by Worcester at the Union Mission on the Grand River in 1835 having been removed to Park Hill in 1837.

[16] Not to be confused with the present town of that name in Alfalfa County, Oklahoma.

[17] Evan Jones (1788–1872), a native of Wales, and his son, John Buttrick Jones (1824–1876), long held a spiritual and temporal influence over the full blood or conservative element of the Cherokee people that amounted to power in tribal affairs. No dry-footed wearers of black, these zealous men plunged eagerly into the life about them and the Cherokee government made them citizens of the tribe and often sought their counsel in public matters. They so mastered the difficult native speech that they could warn sinners of approaching doom and indeed manage all their affairs unhampered by interpreters, a huge advantage which few missionaries of the time took pains or had the wit to seize. Although Methodist competitors were able now and then to dazzle the Indians with the public display of a real bishop and although Presbyterian rivals had better connections in New York and Boston and hence in heaven itself, the first-rate Jones men won and bequeathed to succeeding generations of Oklahoma Baptists a virtual monopoly in rural Cherokee souls.

Hervey Upham (1820–1897), a native of Salem, Massachusetts, learned the printer's craft at the *Christian Watchman* office at Boston and arrived in Indian Territory in 1843, bringing press and type with him, as a missionary of the American Baptist Foreign Mission Society. He resigned in 1851. Upham died near Boerne, Texas, many years stone-blind from an old woman's home-made eye medicine.

The Baptist Mission press was operated intermittently down to the eve of the Civil War. Twelve year old Ned Bushyhead [18] was Hervey Upham's apprentice there in 1844, and no doubt had some small hand in printing the volume described above. John Candy was the printer there in 1855 and Mark Tyger in 1858.

OkU

The constitution and laws of the Cherokee Nation: passed at Tah-le-quah, Cherokee Nation, 1839. Washington: printed by Gales and Seaton. 1840. [*And* Cherokee Baptist Mission, 1844.] [12

107 p. 19 cm.

The combined contents of Nos. 7 and 11 of this bibliography.

A made-up volume. The Gales and Seaton (Washington, 1840) edition of the constitution and 1839 acts forms the first 36 pages. Pages 37–102 were printed from the forms for pp. 3–68 of the Upham (Cherokee Baptist Mission, 1844) edition of the acts of 1840–43, pages and signatures newly numbered to follow the Gales and Seaton volume without break, and two repetitious lines at the bottom of p. 48 deleted. The table of contents of the Upham volume (pp. 69–72) was discarded and a new table (pp. 103–107) printed to cover the contents of the combined volume.

MH-L OkTG Streeter

Laws of the Cherokee Nation, passed at Tahlequah, Cherokee Nation, 1844–5. Tahlequah, printed at the office of the Cherokee Advocate. 1845. [13

26 p. 20 cm.

[18] Edward Wilkerson Bushyhead (1832–1907) was born in the Tennessee part of the old nation of a prominent Cherokee family. His father, Jesse Bushyhead, a Baptist preacher and for several years chief justice of the Cherokee Nation, had given Evan Jones aid in establishing the Baptist Mission in 1839. After his apprenticeship, Ned Bushyhead worked at the *Advocate* office at Tahlequah and later, it is said, at John F. Wheeler's newspaper office at Fort Smith. In 1849 he joined a party of Cherokee crossing the plains to California in search of gold and remained there to become successively newspaper publisher, chief of police at San Diego, and sheriff of San Diego County.

Acts and resolutions of the regular session of October 1844.

500 copies each were ordered printed in English and Cherokee. No copy of the Cherokee edition has been found but there is contemporary evidence that such a volume, a translation by James D. Wofford, was printed at the *Advocate* office in 1845.

The *Cherokee Advocate,* like its Georgia parent, the *Cherokee Phoenix,* was the official newspaper of the Cherokee Nation. It appeared weekly, with several interruptions and with slightly varying captions, from 1844 to 1906. Many acts of the Cherokee council first appeared in its columns and many volumes of the laws issued from its press. The first editor was William Potter Ross or Kanuñtsuwa[19] (1820–1891), a mixed blood Cherokee educated at the College of New Jersey (now Princeton University) and later elected principal chief. A succession of native printers at the *Advocate* office in its early years included John Candy, Mark Tyger, Edward Wilkerson (Ned) Bushyhead, Bird Wilson,[20] Chilly McIntosh,[21] John Spencer, and Arch Stand or Degatâga.

**DSI-E MH-L OkTG Streeter**

**Laws of the Cherokee Nation. Passed at the annual session of the National Council, 1845. Tahlequah: printed at the Cherokee Advocate Office, 1846.** [14

20 p. 18.5 cm.

Acts and resolutions of the regular session of October 1845.

500 copies each were ordered printed in English and Cherokee. No copy of the Cherokee edition has been found but there is contemporary evidence that such a volume, a translation by James D. Wofford, was printed at the *Advocate* office in 1846.

**MH-L Streeter**

[19] That is, osprey or fish-hawk.

[20] Darkly brooding all the way upon some back pay due to him, Wilson one night drove a horse and buggy from Tahlequah to Park Hill, called on the editor, who was night-shirted and just going to bed, pointed a loaded gun straight at him and threatened to blow out his brains on the spot. Sleepily surprised into a promise of payment and thus naturally brought to his senses, the editor flew into a tremendous rage and blazed away at his astonished assailant with both barrels in the very next issue of the paper.

[21] Chilly McIntosh was probably the young Creek Indian known to have served an apprenticeship in 1843 under John F. Wheeler at the *Arkansas Intelligencer* office at Van Buren. He is not to be confused with the well-known Creek chief and Baptist preacher of that name.

[Laws of the Cherokee Nation, passed at the annual session of the National Council, 1846.] [15

[Tahlequah, 1846?]

19 cm.

A volume in the English language, known from a fragment, a single leaf, to have been printed. The Gilcrease Foundation owns a copy of the first leaf of text, pp. [3]/4, the title above being the caption on p. [3]. The two pages on this leaf contain the first three acts of the session, one passed October 12 and two October 14. The volume was printed in late 1846 or early 1847.

*Acts of* 1846, *in Cherokee.* 1847.

[2 *lines in Cherokee*] / 1846. [16

[Tahlequah, 1847.]

19 p. 17 cm. Caption title. Text in Cherokee.

Acts and resolutions of the regular session of October 1846, translated into Cherokee by James D. Wofford.

James Daugherty Wofford or Tsusquanuñnawata[22] (1806–1896?), a cousin of the eminent Sequoya, was the official translator for the *Advocate* from its establishment in 1844 until April 1847. While a student at a Baptist missionary school for Cherokee youth conducted by the Reverend Evan Jones at Valleytown in western North Carolina, he had prepared a Cherokee spelling-book, the second book in the language, which was printed in the Roman alphabet at New York in 1824. He was a member of the national committee in the old nation in Georgia, and after the removal, in which he served as one of two commanders of the largest detachment of emigrants, he was elected to the national council, taking his seat in October 1845. A conservative, and well-versed in the history and traditions of his people, Wofford in his old age was one of the principal informants of James Mooney, the late authority on the Cherokee.

The volume was printed at the *Advocate* office.

Shleppey

Whereas, A communication has been received by the National Council from the Acting Chief, enclosing communications from the Cherokee Agent, to him, dated September 16th, 1848; also

[22] That is, worn-out blanket.

one from the Commissioner of Indian Affairs to Jno. Ross, Principal Chief . . . [Tahlequah, 1848.] [17

Broadside. 25 cm. Without caption, the title above being the first three lines of text.

The resolution, passed by the national council October 17, 1848, touches the proposed removal from Carolina to the Cherokee Nation of a small remnant of the once powerful Catawba tribe.

OkTG

There is some contemporary evidence that a volume was printed at Tahlequah at the *Advocate* office in 1849 which contained, in English, the acts and resolutions of the regular sessions of 1847 and 1848 but no copy has been found.

Laws of the Cherokee Nation: adopted by the Council at various periods. Printed for the benefit of the Nation. Cherokee Advocate Office: Tahlequah, C. N. 1852. [18

179, 248 p. 17.5 cm. Signatures: [1], 2–5, [6], 7–35, each 6 leaves; 4 leaves without signature marks.

The second part of the volume has its own title-page, which reads as follows: The constitution and laws of the Cherokee Nation: passed at Tahlequah, Cherokee Nation, 1839–51. Tahlequah, Cherokee Nation: 1852.

Constitutions of 1827 and 1839, act of union, collected acts and resolutions through the regular session of October 1851, and collected laws of the Western Cherokee or Old Settlers.

This is perhaps the most important single volume in the fields of Cherokee law and history. Luckily, many copies have been preserved, and they are widely distributed and easily accessible.

The Western (or Arkansas) Cherokee, known after they were joined in Indian Territory about 1838 by the main body of the tribe as Old Settlers to mark them from the newcomers, had been persuaded in 1817 by the United States government to exchange their old homes in the East for a wilderness in northwestern Arkansas officially considered worthless and therefore freely conveyed to them and their heirs in fee simple forever. Under the government's liberal policy in such matters the new owners (and their heirs) were conceded the diminishingly undisturbed possession and improvement of this tract for a whole decade or more before they were deprived of it in favor of encroaching Christian whites whose bowie-knives and a flair for night arson conferred upon them a prior and exclusive right to Indian lands tardily seen to be fertile and now providentially cleared, stocked, and fenced.

The collected laws of the Western Cherokee, officially printed here in English and in the following volume in Cherokee, include one adopted orally at Dardanelle Rock, at the present Dardanelle, Arkansas, in 1820 but not reduced to writing until some time later. Their earliest regularly enacted written law appears to have been one, here printed, adopted by the council September 11, 1824, "at John Smith's[23] on Piney Creek" in the southeastern part of the present Johnson County, Arkansas, establishing the executive department of their government.

Amos Kendall, in presenting at Washington in 1846 a claim of the Western Cherokee against the United States, gave the following account of the beginning of their government:

> In that year [1824] a general council was held by the western Cherokees for the purpose of framing a written constitution and adopting a code of laws. After several fruitless efforts, the council appointed Daniel Brown to prepare a form of government and a code of laws, to be reported to an adjourned meeting a month thereafter. He faithfully performed the duty, and his reports were unanimously adopted. The new government had three branches—the legislative, executive, and judiciary. The legislative consisted of a national committee and a national council elected for one year; the executive, of a principal chief and an assistant principal chief, who was *ex officio* president of the council, both elected for four years; the judiciary consisted of a supreme court, circuit, and district courts, the judges of the supreme and circuit courts chosen by the council for four years, and the judges of the district courts for one. The laws then enacted were few, simple, and plain, well adapted to the condition of the western Cherokees. The government went immediately into operation.[24]

The Western Cherokee were politically reunited with the main body of the tribe when they signed the act of union in 1839 but they remained a dissident faction for many years.

[23] John Smith was one of the leading men of the Western Cherokee. He was a signer of the treaty of 1817.

[24] *30th Congress, 2nd Session, Senate Executive Document 28* (1846), 72.

*Compilation, in Cherokee.* 1852.

[12 *lines in Cherokee*] / [*thick-thin rule*] / [3 *lines in Cherokee*] / [*short rule*] / 1850. [19

[Tahlequah, 1852.]

148, 31, 276 p. 17.5 cm.

The contents of the preceding volume, translated into Cherokee.

The printing of the volume was begun at the *Advocate* office in 1850 and completed in 1852.[25] The chief printers were the seasoned John Candy and Mark Tyger. Tyger's Cherokee name, Damaga,[26] is the only printer's name on the Sequoyan title-page; Candy seems to have joined in the work after it was under way and after the real size of the undertaking had become apparent.

The translation into Cherokee of those parts of the volume not reprinted from earlier translations was made by Hercules T. Martin and Joseph Blackbird although Martin is the only translator named on the Sequoyan title-page.

The full blood Hercules Terrapin Martin or Tsunigutlâhiduñ[27] (1817?–1867), council interpreter and from 1847 to 1851 clerk of the council, was considered one of the best Cherokee translators of his day. He was an active member of the Old Settler party and at one time the secretary of its council. In 1840 he was appointed postmaster at the Cherokee agency adjacent to Fort Gibson. Martin served as secretary of the important convention of the Confederate Indians and the wild tribes held in May 1865 at Camp Napoleon on the Washita River. He was born near Guntersville, Alabama, and in his youth attended the Choctaw Academy[28] in Kentucky.

[25] A big job for a country newspaper office, the simultaneous production of this volume and the preceding one taxed the capacities of the *Advocate* so heavily that publication of the newspaper had to be suspended for four months towards the end of the work.

[26] Some little confusion has arisen from the circumstance that Damaga, which means horsefly, was also the Cherokee name of a certain Horsefly (d. 1848?), a full blood whose son James Horsefly (1840–1908) served in 1878 as a translator for the *Advocate* and later as a member of the council and as council interpreter.

[27] That is, hobbled, like a horse.

[28] The Choctaw Academy, or Colonel Johnson's Indian School, as it was sometimes called, was established in 1825 at Great Crossings, near Georgetown, Kentucky, by Richard Mentor Johnson, the reputed slayer of Tecumseh and later vice-president of the United States under Van Buren. The chief patrons of the school were the Choctaw and Chickasaw, who sent there at tribal expense so many of their promising boys that the school roll amounts almost to an index of their subsequent leaders. Smaller numbers were sent by the Cherokee, Creek, and Seminole tribes and a few even by the Omaha, Potawatomi, Quapaw, and Miami. There were the classic and no doubt well-founded complaints of their elders that the boys neglected their studies in favor of gaming and wenching and

Joseph Blackbird or Diganugâwisgi[29] (d. 1854), who was known also as Joseph B. Bird, succeeded James D. Wofford in 1847 as official translator for the *Advocate.* Blackbird had served as interpreter for Methodist circuit riders in the Cherokee Nation in the East before the removal of the tribe. In 1843 and 1844 he was solicitor of Skin Bayou District.

Although sixty copies of the English edition have been found, only three complete examples of this Cherokee version are now known. Almost without exception, the Indian language versions of the laws are rarer than the English. There are good reasons for this. In the councils of the civilized tribes, although deliberations were bilingual, the laws were drafted and adopted in English and they were first printed in that language. Tribal officials, court officers, Indian agents, and indeed almost every one who occasion to consult the laws relied upon the English text. Translations into the native tongue were made later, often months afterward, and printed in smaller numbers primarily for those full bloods sufficiently interested to want a copy of the laws but unable to read English; and few full bloods had means of housing for very long or handing down any of the books that came their way.

DLC DSI-E OkTG

Laws of the Cherokee Nation; passed at the annual sessions of the National Council of 1852–3. Published by authority. Cherokee Advocate print. Tahlequah, C. N.: 1853. [20

33 p. 19.5 cm.

Acts and resolutions of the regular October sessions of 1852 and 1853.

500 copies were ordered printed.

OkTG

*Acts of* 1852 *and* 1853, *in Cherokee.* 1854.
[*6 lines in Cherokee*] / [*row of colons*] / [*1 line in Cherokee, ending with the date* 1854] [21

[Tahlequah, 1854.]

34 p. 20 cm.

---

that they brought home chiefly affected manners and fancy pants. The school was closed in 1845, a short time after the Choctaw Nation withdrew its support and established its own schools at home.

[29] That is, one who keeps on putting something out of a house or a field or a box, and so forth. Blackbird's name uniformly so appears in official literature printed in Cherokee. To members of his own family, however, he seems to have been known as Tlanusi, a very old name in the tribe and a Cherokee word which means water leech.

The contents of the preceding volume, translated into Cherokee.

500 copies were ordered printed. The volume was printed at the *Advocate* office.

**NN OkTG**

Laws of the Cherokee Nation; passed at the annual sessions of the National Council of 1854–'55. Published by authority. Cherokee Advocate print. Tahlequah, C. N.; 1855. [22

29 p. 17 cm.

Acts and resolutions of the regular October sessions of 1854 and 1855.

**OkTG**

*Acts of* 1854 *and* 1855, *in Cherokee.* 1856.
[6 *lines in Cherokee*] / [*row of colons*] / [1 *line in Cherokee, ending with the date* 1856] [23

[Tahlequah, 1856.]

30 p. 17 cm.

The contents of the preceding volume, translated into Cherokee.

The volume was printed at the *Advocate* office.

**OkTG**

Proceedings of the Cherokee convention. [Tahlequah, 1861.] [24

Broadside. 50 cm. 4 columns. Text in English and in Cherokee.

An address by Principal Chief John Ross to a convention of the Cherokee people August 21, 1861, and resolutions of the convention. The resolutions empowered officials of the Cherokee Nation to negotiate an alliance with the Confederate States of America.

The president of the convention, which met at Tahlequah, was Joseph Vann or Diyâli[30] (1798–1877), of Webbers Falls, a Cherokee mixed blood of Scottish descent, at one time an associate justice of the supreme court, and long a leader in tribal affairs. As a boy Judge Vann fought in the Creek War under General Jackson and took part in the Battle of Horseshoe Bend. A prosperous planter and merchant, he owned a good many slaves but, like Principal Chief John Ross, he opposed secession—or, more properly

[30] That is, roasting ear. Judge Vann's name is often found in official literature printed in Cherokee as Tsâwa (that is, Joseph) Diyâli.

in the case of an Indian tribe, repudiation of treaties with the United States.

DNA

Message of the Principal Chief of the Cherokee Nation, together with the declaration of the Cherokee people of the causes which have led them to withdraw from their connection with the U. States. [Tahlequah, 1861.] [25

11 p. 20.5 cm.

The declaration, adopted in convention at Tahlequah October 28, 1861, amounts to an ordinance of secession; it repudiated all treaties with the United States and ratified the alliance contracted earlier that month with the Confederate States of America.[31] Albert Pike (1809–1891), who negotiated the treaty for the Confederate States, asserted in 1866 that he himself, at the request of Principal Chief John Ross, wrote the text of the declaration.

The presiding officer of the convention was Thomas Pegg or Ayuñadegi[32] (1802?–1866), an early emigrant who had been active in Western Cherokee affairs before the arrival of the main body of the tribe. He was at various times senator from Saline District, associate justice of the supreme court, member of the national committee, and tribal delegate to Washington. As president of the national committee he was ex officio principal chief in 1862 and 1863 during the forced absence of Principal Chief John Ross. Judge Pegg served as a major in the Confederate army for a short time after the outbreak of the war but when Union forces overran the Cherokee country he went over with many of his fellows to the Union side.

In addition to the copy noted below, there is one other, in private hands.

DNA

Memorial of the delegates of the Cherokee Nation to the President of the United States, and the Senate and House of Representatives in Congress. Washington Chronicle print, 1866. [26

12 p. 23 cm. Printed wrappers.

[31] The Cherokee Indians, who had nothing to gain in a struggle for states' rights, suffered so greatly in the Civil War that the end of hostilities found their numbers reduced by a third and their country a blackened and desolated waste.

[32] That is, one who plunges in and swims forward.

Pages 11 and 12 contain three acts of the national council of the loyal Cherokee government passed in February 1863 in special session within Union lines at Cowskin Prairie. The first repudiated the treaty of alliance with the Confederate States and reasserted allegiance to the United States. The second removal disloyal, or Confederate, officeholders. The third emancipated negro slaves.

Cowskin Prairie is a low stretch of land lying on the Missouri border, in the northeastern part of the former Cherokee Nation.

DLC MH OkTG OkU-P

Communication of the delegation of the Cherokee Nation to the President of the United States, submitting the memorial of their National Council, with the correspondence between John Ross, Principal Chief, and certain officers of the rebellious states. Washington: Gibson Brothers, printers. 1866. [27

48 p. 22.5 cm. Printed wrappers.

Among the documents on Confederate Indian diplomatic and military history are an act of the Cherokee council of November 7, 1865, and an act of the Chickasaw legislature of January 5, 1861.

DLC NN OkTG

Amendments to the constitution of the Cherokee Nation, adopted Nov. 26, 1866. Washington: 1867. [28

7 p. 13.5 cm. Wrapper title.

The proclamation of the principal chief calling a convention for November 26 and four amendments adopted November 28. The amendments, fruit of Confederate defeat, deal chiefly with the new problems of shrunken boundaries and liberated negro slaves.

The president of the convention, which was held at Tahlequah, was the mixed blood Riley Keys or Kanasgawi[33] (1813–1884), a prominent member of the Old Settler party and successively district judge, associate justice and chief justice of the supreme court, and tribal delegate to Washington. There is testimony that Judge Keys took a hand as a young man in the murder of Elias Boudinot.[34]

OkTG

[33] That is, snipe.

[34] *Chronicles of Oklahoma,* XII (1934), 24.

**Laws of the Cherokee Nation, passed during the years 1839–1867, compiled by authority of the National Council. St. Louis: Missouri Democrat print, corner Fourth and Pines sts. 1868.** [29

208 p. 23 cm.

Collected laws in force, selected special acts and resolutions, and the acts and resolutions of the regular session of November and the extra session of December 1867.

500 copies were ordered printed.

The volume was compiled and edited by the mixed blood William Penn Boudinot or Kâlanu[35] (1830–1898), a son of the noted Elias Boudinot. Educated in the East during the troubled years that followed the assassination of his father in 1839, Boudinot returned to the Cherokee Nation to become several times editor of the *Advocate,* a lieutenant colonel serving with Indian troops in the Confederate army, and long a prominent actor in tribal affairs.

**The act of union between the Eastern and Western Cherokees, the constitution and amendments, and the laws of the Cherokee Nation, passed during the session of 1868 and subsequent sessions. Tah-le-quah: Cherokee Nation. National press.—Edwin Archer, printer. 1870.** [30

100 p. 18.5 cm.

The act of union, the constitution and amendments, and the acts and resolutions of the extra session of September and the regular session of November 1868, and the regular session of November and the extra session of December 1869.

The volume was printed at the *Advocate* office.

Edwin Archer (1817–1893), born in New York City and of Irish descent, suddenly abandoned training for Catholic orders, it is said, and arrived in the Cherokee Nation in 1844 as a school teacher and a permanent Protestant. He joined John Candy at the mission press at Park Hill in 1846. From 1847, when he married a daughter of Joseph (Little Joe) Vann, a prominent mixed blood Cherokee, Archer was in charge of the press until 1860, when northern missionary activities came to an abrupt

[35] Kâlanu, formerly a war title in the tribe, is a word meaning raven. It is the name by which Sam Houston was known to the full bloods when he lived with the Cherokee. Boudinot's name sometimes appears in official literature printed in Cherokee as Kâlanu Galagina, Galagina having been the Cherokee name of his father.

end. His name appears on Sequoyan title-pages as Gulatsi, which is merely a Cherokee attempt at the name Archer.

*Compilation, in Cherokee.* 1871.

[*6 lines in Cherokee*] / [*filet*] / [*2 lines in Cherokee*] / 1871. [31

[Tahlequah.]

310 p. 21 cm.

The contents of the two preceding volumes, translated into Cherokee. Two temporary acts of the regular session of November 1868 are omitted; the translation is otherwise complete.

The volume was printed at the *Advocate* office.

**DLC DSI-E ICN MH-L MiU-L NN NNB OkHi OkTG**

Laws and joint resolutions of the National Council: passed and adopted at the regular and extra sessions of 1870. National Printing Office: Tahlequah, Cherokee Nation. 1871. [32

60 p. 16 cm.

Acts and resolutions of the regular session of November and the extra session of December 1870.

300 copies were ordered printed. The volume was printed at the *Advocate* office.

**CSt DLC MH-L OkHi**

Laws and joint resolutions of the National Council: passed and adopted at the regular and extra sessions of 1871. Frank J. Dubois, printer: Tahlequah, Cherokee Nation. 1872. [33

42 p. 16.5 cm.

Acts and resolutions of the regular session of November and the extra session of December 1871.

The volume was printed at the *Advocate* office. 500 copies were ordered printed.

**C DJ DLC ICLaw MH-L NNB OkHi OkTG OkTahT**

*Acts of* 1870–72, *in Cherokee.* 1872.

[3 *lines in Cherokee*] / [*filet*] / [*6 lines in Cherokee*] / [*filet*] / [*2 lines in Cherokee*] / 1872. [34

[Tahlequah.]

151 p. 17.5 cm. Text in Cherokee.

The contents of Nos. 32, 33, and 35 of this bibliography, translated into Cherokee.

The volume was printed at the *Advocate* office.

**CSmH CU-Law DSI-E ICN NN OkTG**

**Laws and joint resolutions of the National Council, passed and adopted at the extra and regular sessions of 1872. John Doubletooth, printer: Tahlequah, Cherokee Nation, 1873.** [35

61 p. 17 cm.

Acts and resolutions of the extra session of October, the regular session of November, and the extra session of December 1872.

The volume was printed at the *Advocate* office.

The printer John Doubletooth or Tali Diganuñdâgi[36] was a full blood Cherokee who had served in the Civil War as a sergeant in Captain James Vann's company (Co. K) of the Third Regiment, Indian Home Guards, and later as solicitor of Going Snake District. He was murdered in 1875.

**C DLC ICLaw MH-L NNB NNLI OkHi OkTG OkTahT**

**Constitution and laws of the Cherokee Nation. Published by authority of the National Council. St. Louis: R. & T. A. Ennis, stationers, printers and book binders, 118 Olive Street. 1875.** [36

284, [vii] p. 22 cm.

The act of union, the constitution and amendments, a civil and criminal code in force after November 1, 1875, and general laws not inconsistent with the code; the compact of 1843 with the Creeks and Osage, the treaty of 1867 with the Delawares, and the agreement of 1869 with the Shawnee.

The volume was compiled and the laws codified by a commission composed of W. P. Boudinot, D. H. Ross, and J. A. Scales. Boudinot has already been noticed as the compiler of No. 29 of this bibliography.

The mixed blood Daniel Hughes Ross or Ahuñma[37] (1822–1891), in his youth an enthusiastic marksman and bear hunter, was a nephew of Principal Chief John Ross and long a prominent Cherokee merchant. He was several times editor of the *Advocate*.

[36] Literally, two teeth. The name appears several times in official literature printed in Cherokee as Tsegi (that is, Jack) Tali Diganuñdâgi.

[37] The meaning of the word has been lost.

# LAWS

OF THE

# CHEROKEE NATION,

PASSED BY THE

## National Committee and Council.

*PRINTED BY ORDER OF THE COMMITTEE AND COUNCIL.*

KNOXVILLE,

PRINTED AT THE KNOXVILLE REGISTER OFFICE BY

*HEISKELL & BROWN*

1821.

Title Page of No. 1

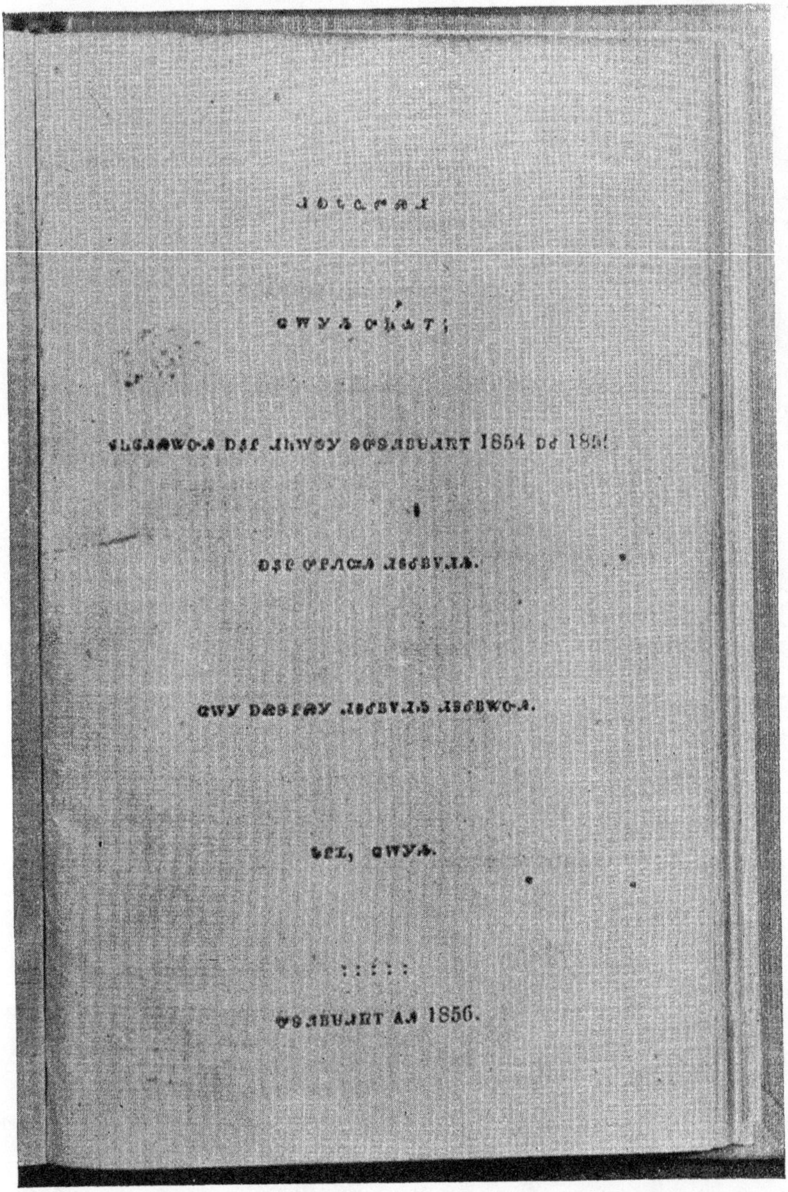

Title Page of No. 23

Joseph Absalom Scales or Digaduñdi[38] (1832–1901), who had three-fourths Cherokee blood, served in the Confederate army as a major on the staff of General Stand Watie. It is said that he held at one time or another every important office in the Cherokee government except that of principal chief.

*Code, in Cherokee.* 1875.

[*5 lines in Cherokee*] / [*filet*] / [*1 line in Cherokee*] / [*cut, seal of the Cherokee Nation*] / [*filet*] / [*3 lines in Cherokee*] / 1875. [St. Louis.] [37

233, v p. 21.5 cm.

The contents of the preceding volume, translated into Cherokee.

A young Cherokee printer, Elias Cornelius Boudinot, Jr. (1854–1896),[39] the son of William Penn Boudinot, one of the compilers, journeyed to St. Louis to supervise the printing of this volume and the preceding one. Presumably he set the type for the Cherokee version. Boudinot learned the printer's craft at the *Advocate* office at Tahlequah and later was twice editor of the paper.

Laws and joint resolutions of the National Council. Passed and adopted at the regular session of 1876. Geo. W. McFarlin, public printer. "Cherokee Advocate" print. 1877. [Tahlequah.] [38

[2], 52, 4 p. 23 cm. Printed wrappers. Errata slip.

Acts and resolutions of the regular session of November 1876.

500 copies each were ordered printed in English and Cherokee. No copy of a Cherokee edition has been found.

The printer, George Washington McFarlin, born in Louisiana in 1849, lived in the Cherokee Nation as a squaw man, that is, an Indian citizen by marriage. One of the early Oklahoma "boomers," he ran at Vinita from 1878 to 1881 a newspaper which advocated the opening of Indian Territory and the future Oklahoma Territory to white settlement. Falling

[38] That is, balance scales. Mr. Long tells me that with the Eastern Cherokee the word is also used for fishing pole.

[39] Boudinot's name appears on later Sequoyan title-pages as Kanelisa (that is, Cornelius) Galagina. Galagina was the Cherokee name of Elias Boudinot, his noted grandfather. Young Boudinot was given his Christian name in honor of his uncle, Elias Cornelius Boudinot or Tsugânuñduñ (1835–1890), an editor and lecturer and an early advocate of the opening of Indian Territory and the future Oklahoma Territory to railroads and white settlers.

in 1879 under the spell of his own editorials, he led several parties of intruders from Kansas into the unassigned lands. At some time in the early 1880's McFarlin removed to Arizona Territory where he continued in newspaper work, at first as a publisher at Wilcox and later as an itinerant printer at Yuma and elsewhere. He spent his last years at Tombstone and it is thought that he died there about 1910.

DIA KHi MH-L OkHi OkTG WHi

Laws and joint resolutions of the National Council. Passed and adopted at the regular sessions of the National Council, of 1876, 1877 and extra session of 1878. 1878: Printed by authority of National Council. [Tahlequah.] [39

52, 4, 46, 3–18, iv p. 22.5 cm. Errata slip.

Acts and resolutions of the regular November sessions of 1876 and 1877 and the extra session of January 1878.

For the first part (pp. [1]–52, [1]–4) of this volume the printer used copies of the preceding volume, discarding the printed wrappers and the title-page. To this he added the newly printed acts and resolutions of November 1877 and January 1878 and a new title to govern the whole.

The volume was printed at the *Advocate* office.

DIA ICLaw Ia-L MoS OkHi OkTG PPB T

Penal law. (Published by authority.) An act for the protection of the public domain, and in relation to intruders upon the same. [Tahlequah, 1878.] [40

Broadside. 33 cm. 2 columns.

Headed: Weekly Advocate. Published every Saturday by the Cherokee Nation. Official journal of the Nation. Saturday, Dec. 28, 1878.

The act was approved by the principal chief December 12, 1878.

A quasi-extra number of the newspaper, the leaf bears the following note at the end: This being Christmas week, and according to a long usage, we did not intend to issue any paper this week; but a penal law over which we had no control compels us to "publish" this. Christmas gift!

Numerous laws of the more advanced tribes were published in contemporary newspapers and more than one, probably, appeared in extra numbers.

OkTG

**Compiled laws of the Cherokee Nation published by authority of the National Council. Tahlequah, I. T.: National Advocate print. 1881.** [41

370, [vi] p. 23 cm.

The act of union, the constitution and amendments, compiled statutes, and a selection from the acts of the regular November sessions of 1879 and 1880; the compact of 1843 with the Creeks and Osage, the treaty of 1867 with the Delawares, the agreement of 1869 with the Shawnee, excerpts from the 1833, 1835, 1846, and 1866 treaties with the United States, and a land patent issued by the United States to the Cherokee Nation in 1838.

1000 copies were ordered printed.

The volume was compiled by John Lynch Adair or Ustinâluñti[40] (1828–1896), a Cherokee mixed blood of Irish descent born in the old nation in Georgia before the emigration. Adair journeyed to California in 1849 in search of gold and returned, without it, in 1853. He was at various times clerk of the Cherokee senate, tribal delegate to Washington, boundary commissioner, and editor of the *Advocate* and of newspapers at Vinita.

*Revised statutes, in Cherokee.* 1881.

[*6 lines in Cherokee*] / 1881. [42

[Tahlequah.]

335, vii p. 22.5 cm.

The contents of the preceding volume, translated into Cherokee by Hiram Terrell Landrum or Nuñwâtiya Igayiduñha[41] (d. 1896), a Cherokee farmer who served at various times as sheriff of Saline District, circuit judge, member of the senate, and national delegate to Washington.

**Senate resolution. Rules for the regulation of the order of business in the Senate. Tahlequah, November 10th, 1881. [Tahlequah, 1881.]** [43

4 p. 22.5 cm. Caption title.

The rules were ordered printed in English and in Cherokee but no copy of the Cherokee version has been found.

**OkU-P**

[40] That is, bushy or brushlike hair. Adair's name often appears in official literature printed in Cherokee as Tsani (that is, John) Ustinâluñti.

[41] The name can not now be satisfactorily translated. The first part of it embodies a reference to pure or true or real medicine.

**Rules for the government of the National Council.** Adopted at its regular session, November, 1883. [Tahlequah, 1883.] [44

Broadside. 33 cm.

A regular act, of 10 sections.

**OkHi**

**An act in relation to minerals.** [Tahlequah, 1883.] [45

Broadside. 26.5 cm. 3 columns.

The act was approved by the principal chief December 15, 1883.

**DLC**

**Mineral law.** [Tahlequah, 1884.] [46

Broadsheet. 40.5 cm.

The act, approved December 12, 1882, is printed in 2 columns. On the verso of the leaf is the printed form of a mining license.

**OkHi OkTG**

**Laws and joint resolutions of the Cherokee Nation,** enacted during the regular and special sessions of the years 1881–2–3. Published by authority of an act of the National Council. E. C. Boudinot, Jr., printer. Tahlequah, Cherokee Nation, 1884. [47

176 p. 23 cm.

Acts and resolutions, some abbreviated and others of a temporary nature probably omitted, of the regular session of November and the extra session of December 1881, the regular session of November and the extra session of December 1882, and the extra session of May and the regular session of November 1883.

The volume was printed at the *Advocate* office. 500 copies were ordered printed.

**DLC ICLaw MH-L MiU-L MnU-L NN NNB OkHi OkTG**

*Acts of* 1881–83, *in Cherokee.* 1884.

[9 *lines in Cherokee*] / [*filet*] / [2 *lines in Cherokee*] / 1884. [Tahlequah.] [48

154 p. 23 cm.

The contents of the preceding volume, translated into Cherokee.

The volume was printed at the *Advocate* office. 500 copies were ordered printed.

**MH-L MnU-L MoS NN OkMu OkTG**

Laws Cherokee Nation. (Extra session, 1884.) [Tahlequah, 1884.] [49

[3] p. 21.5 cm. Wrapper title.

An appropriation act passed and approved December 12, 1884.

OkHi

Compiled laws of the City of Downingville, Cherokee Nation. Published by authority of the City Couneil [*sic*]. Downingville, I. T. Indian Chieftain job print, 1884. [50

[2], 39 p. 22.5 cm.

Laws and ordinances passed by the council in November and December 1883.

Downingville was incorporated by the Cherokee council in 1873. The town was popularly known as Vinita, a name later made official.

DIA

Rules for the regulation of the order of business of the Senate. [Tahlequah, 1885.] [51

4 p. 18 cm. Wrapper title.

The rules are not dated but from a contemporary manuscript note on the copy here described it appears that they were adopted at the regular session of 1885.

OkU-P

An act to create a joint commission to determine claims to citizenship of freedmen under the 9th article of the treaty of 1866. [Tahlequah, 1886.] [52

6 p. 20.5 cm. Caption title.

The act was approved December 11, 1886.

OkTG OkU-P

Mineral law. [Tahlequah, 1887.] [53

Broadsheet. 40 cm.

The act, approved December 15, 1883, is printed in 2 columns. On the verso of the leaf is the printed form of a mining license.

OkHi

Laws and joint resolutions of the Cherokee Nation, enacted by the National Council during the regular and extra sessions of 1884–5–6. Published by authority of the National Council. E. C. Boudinot, Jr., printer. Tahlequah, Cherokee Nation. 1887. [54

99, iii p. 23 cm. Printed wrappers.

Acts in force of the regular November sessions of 1884 and 1885, the extra session of December 1885, and the extra session of April and the regular session of November 1886. Repealed or inoperative acts, of which a list is given, are omitted.

The volume was printed at the *Advocate* office. 1000 copies were printed.

The mixed blood William Penn Boudinot (1830–1898) was the compiler.

**DJ DLC ICLaw MH-L MiU-L MoSL NNB OkHi OkTG**

*Acts of* 1884–86, *in Cherokee.* 1887.

[7 *lines in Cherokee*] / [*filet*] / [2 *lines in Cherokee*] / 1887. [Tahlequah.] [55

87 p. 23 cm.

The contents of the preceding volume, translated into Cherokee by John Leah Springston or Gâlatsusdii[42] (1845–1929), an attorney who served for several years as translator for the *Advocate* and at other times as district court clerk, district sheriff, council interpreter, clerk of the senate, and national secretary. Springston was but one-sixteenth Cherokee. In the Civil War he served on the Union side in Company I, Third Regiment Indian Home Guards.

The volume was printed at the *Advocate* office. 1000 copies were ordered printed.

**DLC MH-L MnU-L OkTG**

Rules of the Council. [Tahlequah, 1887?] [56

Broadside. 26.5 cm. 3 columns.

23 numbered rules.

**OkHi**

[42] That is, little bones. Springston's name regularly appears in official literature printed in Cherokee as Tsani (that is, John) Gâlatsusdii, although he once stated in an application for inclusion in a special tribal roll that his Indian name was Uniquadi. The word is obscene, not in Cherokee, but when turned into English.

*Council rules, in Cherokee.* 1887?

[1 *line in Cherokee.*] [57

[Tahlequah, 1887?]

Broadside. 32 cm. 2 columns.

The foregoing rules, translated into Cherokee.

Shleppey

Rules for the regulating of the order of the business of the Senate. [Tahlequah, 1887.] [58

2 unnumbered leaves, broadside. 32 cm.

According to a manuscript note on the copy here described, the rules were adopted in 1887.

OkHi

Council bill No. 1. An act authorizing the Principal Chief in the name, stead, and behalf of the National Council to dissent from allowance per mile for right of way through the Cherokee domain of the Kansas and Arkansas Valley Railway. [Tahlequah, 1887.]

Broadsheet. 18.5 cm. [59

An adopted act, not a proposed act or bill. The act was passed May 12, 1887.

OkTG

Rules for the government of the Council branch of the National Council. [Tahlequah, 1889?] [60

Broadside. 30.5 cm. 3 columns.

22 numbered rules, followed by the order of business.

The date is conjectured from the circumstance that the copy here described is pasted in the front of a volume containing the manuscript journals of the council sessions of 1889 and 1890.

OkHi

Laws of Cherokee Nation. [Tahlequah, 1890.] [61

3 unnumbered leaves, broadside. 33.5 cm. 3 columns to the page. The title above is the caption on the first leaf. Blind stamp of the seal of the Cherokee Nation in the lower right corner of each leaf.

Ten acts passed in February, November, and December 1888, and November and December 1889.

DLC OkHi OkTG

**Law instructing the several revenue officers of the Cherokee Nation.** [Tahlequah, 1890.] [62

Broadside. 31 cm.

An act approved December 6 and a supplementary act approved December 31, 1890.

OkTG

**Rules for the government** of the Council branch of the National Council. [Tahlequah, 1890?] [63

Broadside. 34 cm.

23 numbered rules, followed by the order of business.

The date is conjectured from the circumstance that the copy here described is pasted in the back of a volume containing the manuscript journals of the council sessions of 1889 and 1890.

OkHi

**Rules and regulations** and order of business, of the Senate. [Tahlequah, 1890?] [64

Broadside. 33 cm.

Rules 1 to 18; additional rules 1–9; revised rules 1–12.

OkHi

*Senate rules, in Cherokee.* 1890?

[4 *lines in Cherokee.*] [65

[Tahlequah, 1890?]

Broadside. 33 cm.

The preceding rules, translated into Cherokee.

MiU-L

**Ordinances of the Town of Tahlequah** instituted by the Town Council, and ordered to be compiled and printed for general information, 1890. Tahlequah: Telephone print, 1890. [66

vii, 62 p. 22.5 cm. Printed wrappers.

Historical sketch of Tahlequah, list of town officers, ordinances authorizing and approving the compilation, an act of the Cherokee council of 1873 incorporating Fort Gibson and Downingville (Vinita) and reincorporating Tahlequah, and revised ordinances of the Tahlequah town council.

The ordinances were compiled and revised by William Penn Boudinot (1830–1898) and Elias Cornelius Boudinot, Jr. (1854–1896), father and son.

**City Clerk's Office, Tahlequah, Oklahoma.**

Road law. [Tahlequah, 1892.] [67

2 leaves, broadside. 29.5 cm. 3 columns to the page. The title above is the caption over the first column of text.

An act approved December 4, 1886, and an amendatory act approved December 4, 1890.

A printed certificate of authenticity at the end is dated March 3, 1892.

**MH-L**

Amendment to the permit law. [Tahlequah, 1892.] [68

Broadside. 25 cm. 3 columns.

The act passed the senate November 22 and the house November 23 and was approved by the principal chief November 25, 1892.

**OkHi**

New jury law. [Tahlequah, 1892.] [69

Broadside. 31 cm. 2 columns.

The act was approved by the principal chief November 28, 1892.

**OkHi OkTG**

New jury law. [Tahlequah, 1892.] [70

Broadside. 30 cm. 3 columns.

Another printing of the preceding act.

**MnU-L**

Constitution and laws of the Cherokee Nation. Published by an act of the National Council. 1892. [Parsons, Kansas, 1893.] [71

426, vii p. 21.5 cm.

The following imprint appears on the verso of the title: The Foley R'y Printing Co., Parsons, Kansas. 1893.

The act of union, the constitution and amendments, and the revised statutes; the compact of 1843 with the Creeks and Osage and the supplemental compact of 1884; the agreement of 1867 with the Delawares, the agreement of 1869 with the Shawnee, excerpts from the 1833, 1835, 1846, and 1866 treaties with the United States, and a land patent issued by the United States to the Cherokee Nation in 1838.

2000 copies were ordered printed.

The mixed blood John Lynch Adair (1828–1896) was the compiler. He has already been noticed as the compiler of No. 41 of this bibliography.

### *Revised statutes, in Cherokee.* 1893.

[8 *lines in Cherokee*] / 1892. [72

[Parsons, Kansas, 1893.]

340, vii p. 22 cm.

The contents of the preceding volume, translated into Cherokee by William Eubanks or Unenudi[43] (1841–1921), a Cherokee quarter blood long interpreter for the national council and translator for the *Advocate* and at one time executive councillor. Eubanks served in the Confederate army as a captain in Stand Watie's Cherokee regiment. He devised and published about 1890 a simplification of the often tedious Sequoyan characters but the language was on its way out and his system did not catch on.

Like the English version, the volume was printed by the Foley Railway Printing Company. 1500 copies were ordered printed.

Memorial and joint-reso[l]utions no [*for* to] the P[r]esident and Congress of the United States on statehood with Oklahoma Territory. [Tahlequah, 1893.] [73

5 leaves, broadside, backed with heavy paper and bradded together, like a law brief. 30 cm. Caption title.

The resolutions of protest passed the senate December 5 and the council December 6 and were approved by the principal chief December 7, 1893.

An ably written document, wretchedly printed, and on the cheapest paper imaginable.

DNA OkTG

[43] That is, cornsilk. Unenudi is an old name in the tribe.

**The nutshell.** Cherokee constitution and the laws and rulings bearing on the autonomy of the Cherokee Nation condensed in a nutshell by Bruton & Norrid, Muldrow, Ind. Ter. Price, 50 cents. Muskogee, Ind. Ter.: The Phoenix Printing Company, 1894. [74

75, iv p. 21.5 cm. Printed wrappers.

Act of union, constitution of 1839 and amendments of 1866, excerpts from treaties, documents touching the work of the Dawes Commission, and a decision of the United States Supreme Court.

Wilson Otho Bruton (1864–1941), one-sixteenth Cherokee, and partner, with William Christopher Norrid, in the law firm of Bruton & Norrid, was at various times clerk of the Sequoyah District, secretary of Principal Chief William C. Rogers, and mayor of Muldrow. He was born at General Stand Watie's winter quarters in the Choctaw Nation whither many Confederate Cherokee families fled at the approach of Union forces.

OkHi

**Ordinances of the Town of Claremore,** instituted by the Town Council and ordered to be compiled and printed for general information, 1894. 1894: "Progress" Book and Job print, Claremore, I. T. [75

51 p. 23 cm.

Claremore was incorporated by the Cherokee council in 1889.

OkHi

**Rules of the Senate.** [Tahlequah, 1895.] [76

Broadside. 31 cm. Text in 3 volumes.

25 numbered rules.

The leaf is not dated but it contains evidence that the rules were adopted at the regular November session of 1895.

Shleppey

**Census bill.** [Tahlequah, 1896.] [77

2 leaves, broadside. 33.5 cm.

An act, approved August 21, 1896, providing for a census of the Cherokee Nation.

OkHi

An act to appropriate and pay certain monies out of monies arising from the sale of the Cherokee Outlet to the freedmen of the Cherokee Nation. Cherokee Nation, Indian Territory. 1896. [Tahlequah.] [78

7 p. 19 cm. Wrapper title.

The act passed the senate March 24 and the council March 26 and was approved by the principal chief March 27, 1896.

The Cherokee Outlet, popularly called the Cherokee Strip, a prairie of six and a half million acres thrown to the plundered Cherokee when it was of no imaginable use to them or to any one else, grew in time so valuable for grazing purposes that land hungry whites resolved, like true Indian givers,[44] to get it back. Their will was accomplished in 1891 when the government, ever anxious to rescue Indians from the curse of cash in the bank, virtually seized the Outlet at half the price offered its owners by a cattle syndicate.

OkTG

Acts of the National Council authorizing and directing the sale of intruder improvements. Tahlequah, I. T. Sentinel print. 1897. [79

11 p. 21 cm. Wrapper title.

Four acts passed in September 1895, December 1895, April 1896, and December 1896, respectively.

MH-L OkHi OkTG

Acts of the National Council authorizing and directing the sale of intruder improvements. Tahlequah Hawkeye print. [Tahlequah, 1897.] [80

12 p. 21 cm.

Another printing of the contents of the preceding volume, together with a list of citizenship cases.

OkHi OkTG

Penal laws of the Cherokee Nation, passed by the National Council and approved for the years 1893–4–5–6. [Tahlequah, 1897.] [81

16 p. 21 cm.

[44] A term of mixed envy and admiration applied in the United States to anyone achieving the businesslike goal inevitably suggested by the discovery that he has conveyed to an Indian something of unsuspected value.

The first and last leaves have the appearance of a wrapper and indeed are so pasted over the back as to serve as one but they must be counted in the pagination.

Eleven acts passed variously in November 1892, January, May, November, and December 1894, December 1895, and December 1896.

**DJ OkHi OkTG OkTahT PPB**

**Penal laws of the Cherokee Nation passed by the National Council and approved for the years 1893–4–5–6. Tahlequah, I. T., Sentinel print, 1898.** [82

14, [2] p. 21.5 cm. Wrapper title. The front wrapper must be counted in the pagination.

Another printing of the contents of the preceding volume.

**MH-L OkHi OkTG OkTahT**

**Rules of the Senate. [Tahlequah, 1899.]** [83

Broadside. 34 cm. 3 columns.

26 numbered rules, signed: E. L. Cookson, W. T. Davis, W. H. Hendricks, Committee.

The following manuscript note appears on the copy here described: Adopted November 7, 1899.

**OkHi**

**An act making disposition of estray property. [Tahlequah, 1900.]** [84

Broadside.

The act was approved November 22, 1900.

**OkTG OkU-P**

**Acts of the National Council authorizing and directing the sale of intruder improvements. [Tahlequah, 1900?]** [85

6 p. 23.5 cm. Wrapper title.

Another printing of the four acts which appeared in Nos. 79 and 80 of this bibliography.

**NN OkHi OkTG**

**Rules for the government of the Council branch of the National Council.** [Tahlequah, 1900?] [86

Broadside. 31 cm.

23 sections, and the order of business.

**OkU-P**

**Rules of the Senate.** [Tahlequah, 1905.] [87

Broadside. 32 cm. 3 columns.

25 numbered rules, signed: C. V. Rogers, Ezekiel Proctor, W. T. Harnage, Committee on rules.

The following manuscript note appears on the copy here described: Adopted by the Senate Committee Nov. 15, 1905. John W. Sharp, Jeff. Muskrat.

**OkHi**

# THE CHICKASAW NATION

The Chickasaw Indians, a Muskhogean tribe formerly living in northern Mississippi and western Alabama, were first observed in 1540 by Hernando de Soto. They were a brave people and their early history is one of constant warfare with neighboring tribes. The steady encroachment of white settlers resulted in 1837 in the removal of the Chickasaw to Indian Territory where they first settled among the Choctaw, to whom they were closely related and whose language, modified by a slight dialect, they shared. As the Chickasaw District of the Choctaw Nation, the tribe was at first represented in the Choctaw council but for some years before the separation of the two tribes in 1855 the Chickasaw had a written constitution of their own and laws touching matters exclusively tribal. They held negro slaves and were allied with the Confederate States of America. One of the so-called Five Civilized Tribes, the Chickasaw became citizens of the United States in 1906 when their own government was dissolved.

Alone of the great southern tribes, the Chickasaw appear to have had no written laws before their removal to the West. Their earliest known written enactment is one adopted December 15, 1844, "by the Chiefs and Commissioners of the Chickasaws in council assembled"; it provided for establishment and regulation of the Chickasaw Academy. There is an unpublished contemporary manuscript copy in the National Archives.

Under the Chickasaw constitutions of 1848 and 1851, which had force only in matters exclusively tribal since the Chickasaw at the time formed a district of the Choctaw Nation and were governed by the Choctaw constitution and laws, legislative authority was exercised by a council which met annually and which was composed of representatives and captains elected by the people.

Executive authority was held by a chief elected by the council and judicial authority by a supreme judge similarly chosen. The 1856 constitution and again that of 1867, which remained in force until dissolution of the Chickasaw government in 1906, vested legislative authority in a bicameral legislature which met annually and whose members were elected by the people, executive authority in a governor similarly chosen, and judicial authority in a supreme court whose members were elected by the legislature.[1]

An act establishing a committee of vigilance, and for other purposes. The better to watch the interest of our nation and the more securely to protect the rights of our people. [Paris, Texas, 1849.]

Broadside. 31.5 cm. [88

The following imprint appears at the end: Printed at the Western Star Office.

The act, passed by "the General Council of the Chief and Captains of the Chickasaws" and approved July 14, 1849, by the chief of the Chickasaw District, is followed by a supplementary act approved July 17.

Paris, Texas, a frontier trading town frequented by the Choctaw and Chickasaw, lay a few miles south of Fort Towson, Choctaw Nation. There was no press or printer in the Chickasaw country until 1854 when a company of natives, of which Jackson Frazier was the president and Benjamin F. Love the secretary, established a short-lived weekly newspaper, the *Chickasaw Intelligencer,* at Post Oak Grove, a tribal meeting-place and pay-ground five or six miles northeast of Fort Washita.

OkTG

Constitution and laws of the Chickasaw Nation, constitution adopted at Tishomingo City, in 1856. Laws passed in 1856 and 1857. J. T. Daviess, printer. Tishomingo City, 1857. [89

76 p. 17.5 cm.

The constitution adopted August 30, 1856, and the acts and resolutions

[1] In setting up their permanent constitutional government, the Chickasaw eschewed the extravagant official nomenclature found in the governments of most Indian tribes. Their executive officer was simply a governor and their lawmaking body a legislature.

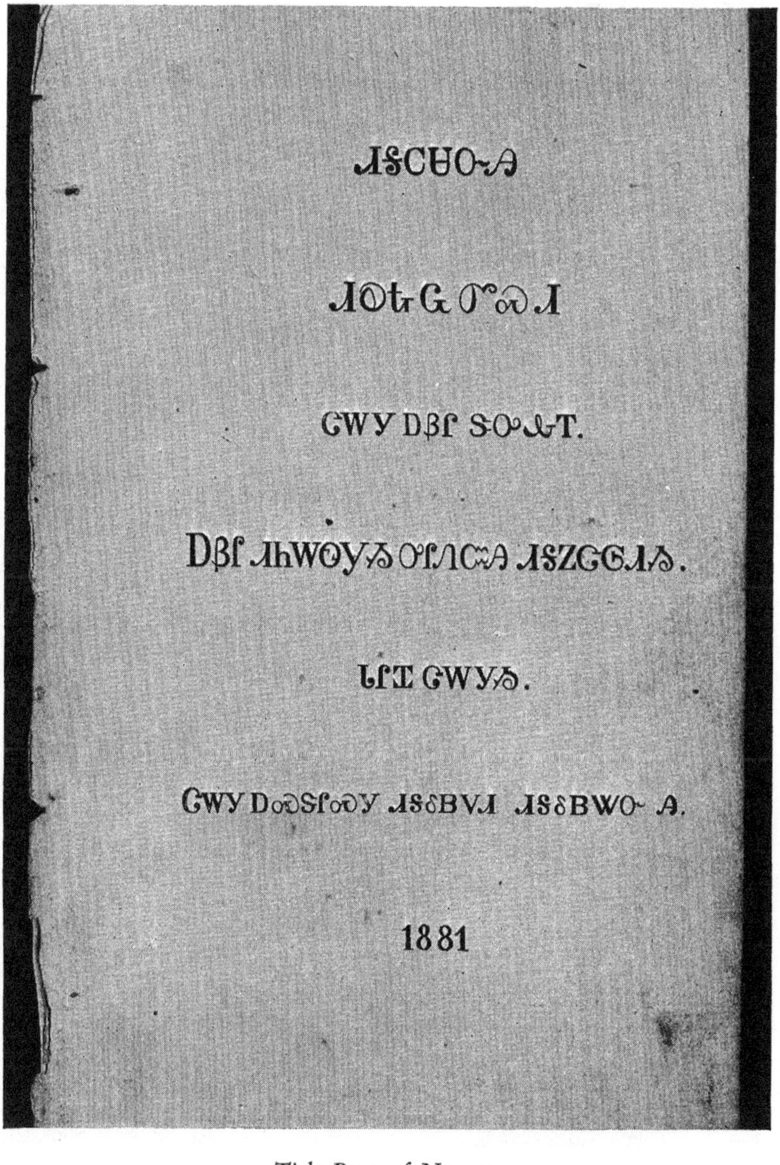


Title Page of No. 42

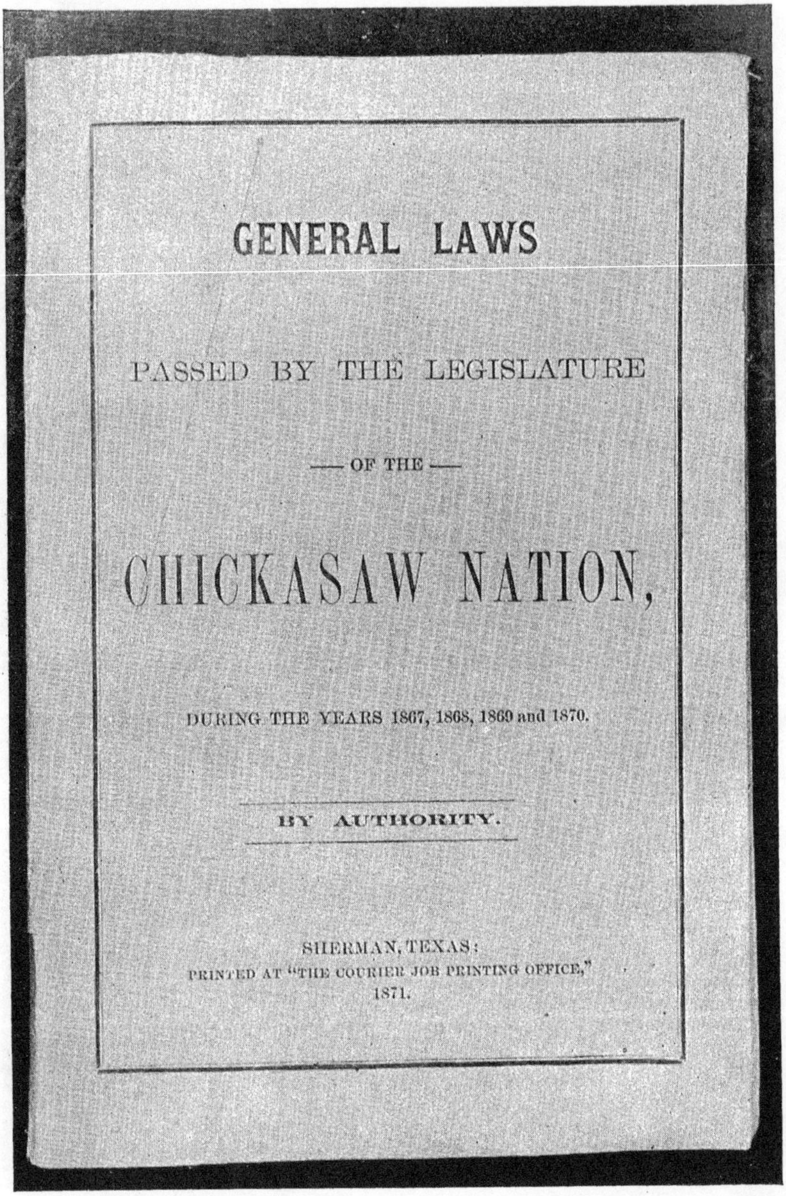

GENERAL LAWS

PASSED BY THE LEGISLATURE

— OF THE —

CHICKASAW NATION,

DURING THE YEARS 1867, 1868, 1869 and 1870.

BY AUTHORITY.

SHERMAN, TEXAS:
PRINTED AT "THE COURIER JOB PRINTING OFFICE,"
1871.

Wrapper Title of No. 94

of the regular session of October 1856 and the called session of August[2] and the regular session of October 1857.

The constitution was drafted by Holmes Colbert (1829–1872), of a mixed blood family long prominent in Chickasaw affairs, and Sampson Folsom (1820–1872), a mixed blood Choctaw, and a Chickasaw citizen by virtue of his marriage into the Colbert family. Folsom took a conspicuous part in the affairs of both tribes and in the Civil War commanded the 1st Choctaw Cavalry Regiment in the service of the Confederate States.

The president of the convention which framed the constitution was the Chickasaw mixed blood Jackson Kemp, a wealthy slaveholder and stock raiser. Kemp served in 1866 as governor pro tem. and in 1867 as president of the senate.

The printer J. T. Daviess edited and printed at Tishomingo City in 1858 and 1859 a short-lived weekly newspaper, the *Chickasaw and Choctaw Herald,* of which Henry McKinney, a mixed blood Chickasaw, was the proprietor.

NNB

The Chickasaw adopted a written constitution in 1846 but the text has not been found. Unpublished manuscript copies, certified by tribal officials, of two other early constitutions are preserved in the National Archives. One was adopted October 13, 1848, "by representatives of the Chickasaw people of the Choctaw Nation assembled in convention at Boiling Springs near Fort Washita in the Chickasaw District" and "read and adopted at the General Council at Boiling Springs" November 4, 1848. The other was adopted October 8, 1851, "by the Chickasaw people at Post Oak Grove."

## Laws of the called session of March, 1858. J. T. Daviess, printer, Tishomingo City. 1858. [90

37 p. 17 cm.

[2] The dog-days session of 1857 was called for the sweltering reconstruction, with loud curses and oaths, of important acts passed in October 1856 whose manuscript originals had been lost, with all his cash, when their custodian, one Henry C. Long, accidentally got drunk for a few days while journeying over into Texas to get them printed. Although doubtless often afterward helpfully reminded of it and freely offered many witty conjectures to which the hard laws of human nature obliged him to lend a respectful ear, Long never managed to throw much light on the loss or, for that matter, on his itinerary. He is thought to have purchased early in the journey a jug or two of Johnny Jump Up, a delicious mixture then a frontier favorite, whose trade name accurately reflected the immediate and diverting effect of the stuff upon those who consumed it.

The only known copy is incomplete, having only the first 26 pages, but there are stubs left to show that it extended to 37 pages, the last few of which were devoted to an index.

Acts and resolutions of the called session of March and the regular session of October 1858.

**MH-L**

An act of October 20, 1858, authorized James Gamble and Joel Kemp, the council interpreters, to translate into Choctaw for printing by J. T. Daviess in an edition of 200 copies the constitution and "all the laws of the Chickasaw Nation." On October 17, 1859, the council continued James Gamble as translator and authorized him to appoint an assistant. No copy of such a translation is known in print or in manuscript. James Gamble was appointed Chickasaw delegate to the Confederate Congress in 1861. In 1862 he commanded a battalion of Chickasaw troops in Confederate service. Joel Kemp (1836–1875) had served in 1855 as president of the council.

Constitution, laws, and treaties of the Chickasaws, by authority. Tishomingo City: printed by E. J. Foster. 1860. [91

232 p. 23.5 cm.

The contents of the two preceding volumes and the acts and resolutions of the extra session of January and the regular session of October 1859, and the treaties with the United States of 1832, 1834, 1852, and 1855, and the 1837 treaty with the Choctaw.

Some copies have a printed slip, pasted down on a blank leaf at front, which reads as follows: It is the intention to establish for the Chickasaws, a National Library. The publisher remits a copy of their first printed volume[3] and solicits in return some suitable contribution. Direct to "E. J. Foster, Fort Smith, Ark." (Care of O. C. Word & co.)

Head Quarters, Dist. Ind. Ter'y. Fort Towson, C. N., Oct. 27th, 1864. The following acts of the Legislature of the Chickasaw Nation, with the proclamation of Governor Pratt, are published for

[3] That is, the first volume that looked like a law book. Foster could hardly have been unaware of the 1857 and 1858 pamphlet laws; indeed he must have used them for printer's copy.

the information of all concerned. By order of Major Gen'l. S. B. Maxey. M. L. Bell, A. A. Gen'l. [Fort Towson, 1864.] [92

Broadsheet. 20 cm. The verso is numbered p. 2.

The conscription act of October 11, 1864, an act of October 8 exempting civil officers of the nation from military duty, and the acting governor's proclamation of October 12 calling for volunteers.

Horace Pratt, for several years a member of the senate and at this time its president, acted as governor during the absence for several months in 1864 of Governor Winchester Colbert. He later served as senate interpreter.

The leaf was printed on the Confederate army press at Fort Towson, Choctaw Nation.

**DNA**

Constitution, laws, and treaties of the Chickasaws. By authority. Fort Smith, Ark.: printed for the Chickasaw Nation, at the Herald Office. John F. Wheeler, printer. 1867. [93

212 p. 22 cm.

The constitution adopted at Camp Harris, Chickasaw Nation, August 16, 1867, and the acts and resolutions of the regular session of October 1856, the extra session of August 1857, the extra session of March and the regular session of October 1858, the extra session of January and the regular session of October 1859, the regular session of October 1860, the extra sessions of January and May and the regular session of October 1861, the regular session of October 1864, the regular session of November 1865, the regular session of November 1866, and the extra session of July 1867; the treaties with the United States of 1832, 1834, 1852, 1855, and 1866; and the treaty of 1837 with the Choctaw.

Inoperative acts are omitted and amended acts printed as amended. An expired act of January 5, 1861, will be found in No. 27 of this bibliography.

Charles P. H. Percy, clerk of the Chickasaw senate, was president of the constitutional convention held at Camp Harris in 1867; later that year he was elected to the council. Percy served in 1868 as speaker of the lower house and as Pontotoc County prosecuting attorney and in 1870 as a delegate to the Okmulgee Council. Camp Harris, whose location is not now known, was probably some convenient camp-ground named in honor of

Cyrus Harris (1817–1888), at the time governor of the Chickasaw Nation.

It will be noticed that several volumes described in this bibliography were printed at Fort Smith, Arkansas. The town grew up at the border army post established in 1817 to quiet hostilities between the Osage and the Western Cherokee and long served the people of Indian Territory as their chief trading resort. The busy Whiskey Road to the Indian country started there. Presiding over the United States district court at Fort Smith, Judge Isaac C. Parker, a sort of practical missionary holding out to frontier evildoers the well-kept promise of a present hell, delivered to the hangman a dreadful number of Indian Territory rascals.

DLC ICLaw KHi MH-L MiU-L MnU-L NNB OkTG

An act of the Chickasaw legislature of September 23, 1868, authorized the governor to make a contract with Joseph Pitchlynn Folsom, a well-known Choctaw lawyer, "for translating [into Choctaw] and printing the Constitution and all the Laws of this Nation," but no such translation is known in print or in manuscript. The contract itself may not have been negotiated; Folsom must have been busy about the time on the Choctaw compilation, No. 122 of this bibliography, printed at New York in 1869.

General laws passed by the Legislature of the Chickasaw Nation, during the years 1867, 1868, 1869 and 1870. By authority. Sherman, Texas: printed at "The Courier Job Printing Office," 1871.

70 p. 22 cm. Printed wrappers. [94

The title above is the wrapper title. The regular title reads as follows: General laws of the Legislature of the Chickasaw Nation; 1867, 1868, 1869 and 1870.

Acts and resolutions of the regular session of October 1867, the extra sessions of February and August and the regular session of September 1868, the regular session of September 1869, and the extra session of May and the regular session of September 1870.

200 copies were ordered printed. Several copies are known which lack the printed wrapper with full title; they are of course incomplete.

The volume was compiled by Josiah Brown or Isitohbi[4] (1835–1905), the national secretary and the holder at one time or another of every im-

[4] That is, white deer.

portant office in the Chickasaw government except those of attorney general and governor.

**OkTG**

*Compilation, in Choctaw.* 1873.

Chikasha okla i kunstitushun micha i nan ulhpisa. Chikasha okla i nan apesa yut apesa tok mak oke. [New York, 1873.] [95

350 p. 22.5 cm.

The constitution, and the acts and resolutions found in the two preceding volumes, repealed acts omitted and amended acts printed as amended, together with the acts and resolutions of the extra session of June, the regular session of September and the extra session of December 1871, the extra session of May and the regular session of September 1872, and the extra session of January 1873, translated into Choctaw, the language used, with only slight modifications, by the Chickasaw. The full text of the acts of June 1871 to January 1873, inclusive, is not known to have been printed in English.

The contents were compiled and translated into Choctaw by the Reverend Allen Wright and the volume was printed, with funds which he himself advanced for the purpose, by the American Tract Society.

Allen Wright or Kiliahote[5] (1826–1885), an influential Choctaw of seven-eighths Indian blood, was born in the old nation in Mississippi. Taught English in the home of a white missionary who discerned promise in him, he was later sent at tribal expense to the East for theological schooling. He returned to his people as a teacher and Presbyterian preacher and he served them at various times as national treasurer, national delegate, treaty commissioner, and principal chief. In the Civil War he was a chaplain with Confederate Choctaw troops. Governor Wright compiled a Choctaw lexicon printed at St. Louis in 1880 and was considered one of the best Choctaw scholars of his day.

**DLC MH-L MiU-L NN OkHi OkTG**

Permit law of the Chickasaw Nation. [Chickasaw Male Academy? 1877.] [96

Broadside. 26.5 cm. 2 columns.

[5] An old name in the tribe. The word may be approximately translated into English as "let us set out now and make a light," but its original significance has been lost. I am here indebted to Governor Wright's granddaughter, Miss Muriel H. Wright, of Oklahoma City, Oklahoma.

The act was approved by the governor October 17, 1876. A printed certificate of authenticity at the end is dated January 25, 1877.

OkTG

Constitution, laws and treaties of the Chickasaws. By authority. Sedalia, Mo.: Sedalia Democrat Company, printers. 1878. [97

231 p. 23 cm.

Constitution, and acts and resolutions of the regular sessions of September 1876 and September 1877; treaties with the United States of 1832, 1834, 1852, 1855, and 1866; and the treaty of 1837 with the Choctaw. The acts of 1876 include a revision of the statutes.

300 copies were ordered printed.

*Compilation, in Choctaw.* 1878.

Chikasha okla i kunstitushun micha i nan ulhpisa chuliti aiena. Chikasha okla i nan apesa yut apesa tok mak oke. Sedalia, Mo. Sedalia Democrat Company, ai ikbi. 1878. [98

256 p. 21.5 cm.

The contents of the preceding volume, translated into Choctaw by Ellis W. Folsom (1829?–1880), a prominent mixed blood Choctaw lawyer. 300 copies were ordered printed.

The *Star-Vindicator* (McAlester, Choctaw Nation) has the following news item in its issue of September 21, 1878: "Judge E. W. Folsom left last Monday for Sedalia to translate the Chickasaw laws, which are being printed there, into the Indian tongue. He expects to be absent about three weeks." Judge Folsom, who was born in the old Choctaw Nation in Mississippi, was part owner of the *Star-Vindicator* and its translator and Choctaw editor. He served as a delegate to the Skullyville convention in 1857 and as a captain in the 1st Regiment Choctaw and Chickasaw Mounted Rifles in the service of the Confederate States. At the time of his death he was supreme judge of the Choctaw Nation.

MH-L MnU-L MoU NNB OkHi OkTG

Laws of the Chickasaw Nation from 1878–1881. Published by authority. [Chickasaw Male Academy, 1881.] [99

18, [1] p. 24.5 cm. Wrapper title.

An act of the regular session of September 1876 omitted from its proper place in No. 97 of this bibliography, and the acts and resolutions of the regular session of October 1878, the extra session of March and the regular session of September 1879, and the regular September sessions of 1880 and 1881.

The Chickasaw Male Academy, a tribal school known also as the Chickasaw Manual Labor Academy, lay three miles southwest of Tishomingo, the Chickasaw capital. The volume was printed by native pupils working under the direction of Joshua M. Harley (1839–1892), the principal. One of the young printers was Hindman Harrison Burris (1862–1940), later the chief compiler of No. 101 of this bibliography and probably the translator of No. 102.

There is some slight evidence in tribal records that the acts of the regular session of October 1878 alone were printed at the *Democrat* office at Sedalia, Missouri, in late 1878 or early 1879 but no copy has been found. Small in number, they probably appeared, in English, on a single leaf or in a very thin pamphlet.

MH-L NNB OkTG

General and special laws of the Chickasaw Nation. Passed during the sessions of the Legislature for the years from 1878 to 1884, inclusive. By authority. Muskogee: Indian Journal Steam Job print, 1884. [100

64, [2] p. 22 cm.

The contents of the preceding volume, the act of September 1876 and one act of September 1879 omitted, and acts and resolutions of the extra session of May and the regular session of September 1882, the regular session of September 1883, and the extra session of May and the regular session of September 1884.

500 copies each were ordered printed in English and Choctaw. No copy of a Choctaw edition has been found.

The Gilcrease Foundation has, besides a copy in the usual sheep, the only copy found in printed wrappers.

DIA DLC DNA ICLaw MH-L MnU-L NNB OkHi OkTG

Constitution, treaties and laws of the Chickasaw Nation. Made and enacted by the Chickasaw Legislature. 1890. Indian Citizen print, Atoka, I. T. [101

343, vii p. 22.5 cm.

The constitution, statutes as revised October 1876, acts in force of the sessions of September 1876 to September 1884, inclusive, and the acts and resolutions of the regular sessions of October 1885, September 1886, September 1887, and September 1888, the extra session of April and the regular session of September 1889, and the extra session of February 1890; the treaties with the United States of 1832, 1834, 1852, 1855, and 1866, and the 1837 treaty with the Choctaw.

1000 copies were ordered printed.

The volume was compiled by a commission of "three persons learned in the law and familiar with the condition and wants of the Chickasaw people," of which Hindman Harrison Burris (1862–1940), a native lawyer, merchant, and farmer, was the chairman. Burris appears on the final roll of his tribe as a full blood. He served at various times as national auditor, speaker of the legislature, and national treasurer.

### *Compilation, in Choctaw.* 1890.

Chikasha okla i kunstitushun micha i nan ulhpisa micha United States a nan itimapehinsa tok mak oke. Chikasha okla i nan apesa yut apesa tok mak oke. 1890. Indian Citizen print, Atoka, I. T.

394, vii p. 22.5 cm. [102

The contents of the preceding volume, translated into Choctaw.

500 copies were ordered printed.

The translation was probably made by Hindman Harrison Burris (1862–1940), the chairman of the commission which compiled the volume. Burris served for some years as interpreter for the Chickasaw supreme court.

**DSI-E MnU-L OkHi OkTG OkU-P**

Chickasaws and Choctaws. Comprising the treaties of 1855 and 1866. The Oklahoma bill, and many laws of especial interest to non-citizens, such as the permit law, the licensed trader law, the stock law, the mining law, the claim law, the lease law; also comprehensive chapters on the history of the Choctaws and Chickasaws, the Chickasaw government, school system, inter-tribal relations, geography of country, status of freedmen, non-citizens, disfranchised citizens, jurisdiction of U. S. court and the allotment question. Sent post-paid to any address in the United States, for fifty cents, by the Chickasaw Chieftain Printing Co., Ardmore, I. T. 1891: Chieftain print, Ardmore, I. T. [103

67, [1] p. 23 cm. Printed wrappers.

Treaties of 1855 and 1866 between the United States and the Choctaw and Chickasaw nations, historical and descriptive sketch of the Choctaw and Chickasaw tribes, extracts from the Oklahoma organic act of May 2, 1890, a discussion of Federal court and allotment questions, and selected laws in force in the Chickasaw Nation.

The volume was compiled by Rezin W. McAdam (1869–1924), the editor and publisher of the *Chieftain* and a native of Virginia. With newspaper experience in New York, Washington City, and western Kansas, McAdam established the *Oklahoma Chief* at Oklahoma City in May 1889 and ran it until September when he removed to Ardmore and started the *Chieftain*. Later he published trade journals at Denver, Colorado, and died there. McAdam compiled, and published in August 1889, four months after the town was settled, the first directory of Oklahoma City.

KHi MH-L MnU-L OkHi

Laws of the Chickasaw Nation, I. T., relating to intermarried and adopted citizens and the rights of freedmen. Compiled by the Chickasaw Commission. Overton Love, chairman. Richard McLish, secretary. M. V. Cheadle. Wm. L. Byrd. H. L. Payne, W. B. Johnson, attorneys. Press of the Chronicle, Ardmore, I. T. [1896.] [104

48 p. 23 cm. Wrapper title, which must be counted in the pagination.

"The laws relating to intermarried and adopted citizens and the negro freedmen in the Chickasaw Nation, enacted since 1856"; and proclamations, affidavits, and official correspondence.

Overton Love (1823–1903), Richard Humphrey McLish (1860–1929), Martin Van Buren Cheadle (1856–1913), and William Leander Byrd (1844–1915) were all prominent Chickasaw mixed bloods. Love was an old Choctaw Academy boy. Byrd was a former governor of the Chickasaw Nation.

Halbert Eleazer Paine (1826–1905) and William Benjamin Johnson (1860–1939) were white lawyers employed to represent the tribe in litigation at Washington. Johnson served from 1898 to 1906 as United States District Attorney for Southern Indian Territory.

MH-L MiU-L MnU-L OkHi OkTG

**Constitution, and laws of the Chickasaw Nation together with the treaties of 1832, 1833, 1834, 1837, 1852, 1855 and 1866. Published by authority of the Chickasaw Legislature by Davis A. Homer. 1899. The Foley Railway Printing Company, Parsons, Kansas.** [105

549, [1], x p. 21 cm.

The reprinted contents of No. 101 of this bibliography, together with the acts and resolutions of the extra session of July and the regular session of September 1890, the extra session of March 1891, the regular session of September 1892, the extra sessions of February and June and the regular session of September 1893, the extra session of January, the regular session of September and the extra session of December 1894, the regular session of September 1895, the extra session of February and the regular session of September 1896, the extra sessions of January and July and the regular session of September 1897, and the extra session of February 1898; an act of Congress regulating tribal courts and providing for surveys, and the text of the so-called Curtis Act of June 28, 1898.

1000 copies were printed.

Davis Aaron Homer or Homma (b. 1864?) was a native Choctaw lawyer and preacher. The *Fort Smith Elevator* of June 22, 1900, has the following note about him: "Rev. D. A. Homer, a full blood Choctaw, who assisted Judge A. R. Durant in translating the Choctaw laws into English,[6] and who, unaided, translated the Chickasaw laws, will go as a missionary to the Comanches, Kiowas and Apaches and translate the hymn book and catechism into the Comanche language. As those tribes have no written language he will have to arrange an alphabet from their signs and hieroglyphics and then teach them the written language."[7]

## *Compilation, in Choctaw.* 1899.

**Chikasha okla i kvnstitushvn micha i nan vlhpisa micha Yonaitet Estets nan ittim apehinsa tok 1832 micha 1834, 1837, 1852, 1855 micha 1866 kvt afoyukka hoke. Mikma holisso illappat toba chi ka Nov. 2, 1897, ash o Chikasha okla i nan apesa yvt apesa tok makoke. Davis A. Homer, akosh anumpa toshole ho. 1899. The**

[6] No. 156 of this bibliography. The translation was made from English into Choctaw, however.

[7] I am indebted for this reference to Miss Hazel E. Beaty and Mrs. O. J. Cook of the Oklahoma Historical Society.

Foley Railway Printing Company, Parsons, Kansas. Ako holisso atoba tuk oke. [106

531, [1], xi p. 21 cm.

The contents of the preceding volume, translated into Choctaw by Davis A. Homer, the compiler.

500 copies were printed.

**CU-Law DLC MH-L MiU-L MnU-L NNB Ok OkTG**

Book of ordinances of the City of Chickasha. Published by authority of a resolution of the City Council and formerly [*sic*] authorized by ordinance number one hundred. Compiled and revised by Alger Melton, of the Chickasha bar. [Chickasha, 1902.]

217 p. 21.5 cm. Printed wrappers. [107

The petition of November 6, 1899, for a charter, and the charter granted February 18, 1902, by the United States Court for the Southern District of Indian Territory; council rules, and the ordinances passed by the council from 1900 to 1902, inclusive.

"The committee on printing are instructed to have printed not less than one hundred copies."

Alger Melton (1874– ), a native of Texas, has long been an attorney at Chickasha. He is a former president of the Oklahoma State Bar.

Chickasha, the present city of that name in Oklahoma, was an important town in the Chickasaw Nation.

**DLC**

# THE CHOCTAW NATION

The Choctaw Indians, a Muskhogean tribe formerly living in middle and southern Mississippi and western Alabama and first encountered in 1540 by De Soto, were essentially an agricultural people and most of the wars in their history were defensive. In the early eighteenth century they entered into friendly relations with the French but later the British won over some of the eastern Choctaw towns and a civil war within the tribe followed. Led by Protestant missionaries and by intelligent mixed bloods of their own number, the peaceable Choctaw made rapid progress in civilization in the early nineteenth century. Threatened with subjection to the laws of Mississippi and their lands coveted by advancing white settlers, the main body of them removed in 1831, 1832, and 1833 to Indian Territory. Slaveholders and southern sympathizers, they allied themselves in 1861 with the Confederate States of America. The second largest group of the so-called Five Civilized Tribes, the Choctaw became citizens of the United States in 1906 when they were deprived of their own government. Their greatest man was Pushmataha (1765–1824), whose clear head and wise view in a critical period kept the Choctaw at peace with the United States.

In the eighteenth century the Choctaw were loosely ruled by a head chief,[1] some of whose power was delegated to second chiefs. By the nineteenth century authority rested in three district chiefs elected by the people. The head chieftainship was nominally revived by the constitution of 1860.

Organized government with written laws began in Mississippi with the adoption of a constitution August 5, 1826, by a council

[1] In a private letter to the bibliographer Dr. John R. Swanton makes the following comment: "In earliest times the head chief's position was very weak, and one early writer claims that the head chieftainship was instituted at the suggestion of the French."

of the chiefs and representatives of the three districts into which the nation was divided. The earliest known regular enactment is one passed the same day appropriating money for building a national council house.[2] The bibliographer owns the unpublished originals, in English and in Choctaw, of both the constitution and the act, in two small manuscript volumes[3] which contain also the acts of the committee and council of the Northeastern District passed in June 1827 and August 1828.

Under the 1826 constitution, legislative authority rested in a council which met annually and whose members were elected by the people, and executive authority in three district chiefs similarly chosen. The 1834 constitution, the earliest adopted after removal of the tribe to the West, assigned judicial authority to a supreme court whose members were appointed by the chiefs. The 1838 constitution added a fourth district chief to the executive department, a fourth district having been created, and set up a military department to be administered by district generals elected by the people. The 1842 constitution made the council a bicameral one. The Skullyville constitution of 1857, whose legality was disputed by the ultraconservative faction of the nation, vested executive authority in a governor elected by the people and judicial authority

[2] The council house was built on the east bank of the Noxubee River in the present Oktibbeha County, Mississippi. The site, afterward long known as Council Bluff, lies about 400 yards above the line between Oktibbeha and Noxubee counties.

[3] In the handwriting of Peter Perkins Pitchlynn (1806–1881), the secretary of the council which adopted the constitution and a member of the committee of the Northeastern District. The manuscripts were purchased by the bibliographer in 1940 from the late Sophia C. Pitchlynn, of Washington, D. C., along with many other important papers saved by her father in his long and distinguished career.

Educated at the University of Nashville, the mixed blood Pitchlynn, who was of English descent, began while still a youth in Mississippi to take a large hand in tribal affairs. He later served as superintendent of the Choctaw Academy in Kentucky, superintendent of schools in the Choctaw Nation, president of the 1850 constitutional convention, tribal delegate to Washington, member of the senate, treaty commissioner, and principal chief. He owned a fine plantation on the Mountain Fork River, at Eagletown, and was one of the largest slaveholders in Indian Territory. His Indian name, Hachotakni, by which it is said the full blood Choctaw always called him, is a word meaning loggerhead turtle. On his first visit to the United States Charles Dickens met Colonel Pitchlynn and was immediately invited to a buffalo hunt, which did not come off, however; Dickens later wrote several friendly paragraphs about him in *American Notes.* The Pitchlynn family long held great power and influence in the Choctaw Nation.

in a supreme court whose members were similarly chosen. The Doaksville constitution of 1860, which represented a compromise between the "progressive" and conservative elements and which, with few changes, remained in force until dissolution of the Choctaw government in 1906, nominally revived the district organizations, continued the bicameral council and the supreme court, and vested executive authority in a principal chief elected by the people.

The constitution and laws of the Choctaw Nation. Park Hill, Cherokee Nation. John Candy, printer. 1840. [108

34, [2] p. 17.5 cm.

Constitution adopted at Nanih Waiya October 3, 1838, and acts of the regular October sessions annually from 1834 to 1839, inclusive, here numbered the 1st to 6th sessions. "Repealed laws are omitted; and amended laws are printed according to amendments."

The volume was compiled and edited and its printing costs borne by the mixed blood David Folsom (1791–1847) to whom the council in 1838 had granted for a period of four years the exclusive privilege of compiling, translating, and publishing the laws. Colonel Folsom, who served from 1826 to 1830 as chief of Mashulatubbi District in the old nation in Mississippi, was one of the earliest Choctaw converts to Christianity and a zealous advocate of education for his people. He collaborated with the missionaries Alfred Wright and Cyrus Byington in preparing the first book in the Choctaw language, a spelling-book published by a missionary society at Cincinnati in 1825.

Nanih Waiya, a mile and a half west of the present Tuskahoma, Oklahoma, served as the capital of the Choctaw Nation from 1834 to 1850. After 1838 the council met in a whitewashed log house built there for the purpose. The place was named for the famous ceremonial mound and tribal center in the old nation in Mississippi.

The bibliographer owns, in the Pitchlynn papers, the unpublished original manuscript, in English, of a constitution adopted June 3, 1834,[4] by representatives of the Choctaw people "assembled in council near Turnbulls Stand on Jacks Fork of Kiameshie where the military road leading from fort Smith to Horse Prarie crosses that stream"—evidently

[4] The earliest constitutional instrument known to have been executed within the borders of the present state of Oklahoma.

at the site agreed upon that year for future council meetings and officially named Nanih Waiya. This constitution superseded that adopted in Mississippi in 1826 and inaugurated Choctaw government in the West.

**DLC MBAt MH-L OkTG Streeter**

*Compilation, in Choctaw.* 1840.

Chahta yakni nan ulhpisa nishkoboka, micha anumpa ulhpisa aiena. Jonathan Cogswell ut Chahta anumpa atosholi tok. Park Hill, Cherokee Nation. John Candy, printer. 1840. [109

39, [1] p. 17.5 cm.

The contents of the preceding volume, translated into Choctaw by Jonathan Cogswell or Ilatochuñbbi,[5] a native missionary and school teacher, who journeyed to Park Hill to see this volume and the preceding one through the printing press. Cogswell was later elected to the Choctaw council. He was a student at the Mayhew Mission School in Mississippi before the removal of the tribe and was one of the early Choctaw converts to Christianity.

There was no printing press or printer in the Choctaw Nation until the establishment at Doaksville in 1848 of a short-lived weekly newspaper, the *Choctaw Telegraph,* of which the mixed blood Daniel Folsom (1813?–1861), a lawyer who had been educated at the Choctaw Academy, was the editor and D. G. Ball, a Doaksville merchant, the printer.

**MBAt MH-L**

The constitution and laws of the Choctaw Nation. Park Hill, Cherokee Nation: Mission press: Edwin Archer, printer. 1847.

107 p. 17 cm. [110

Constitution adopted at Nanih Waiya November 10, 1842, and acts and resolutions of the regular October sessions annually from 1834 to 1846, inclusive, here numbered the 1st to 13th sessions. "Repealed laws are omitted; and amended laws are printed as amended."

300 copies were printed at the expense of Jonathan Cogswell.

Allen W. Carney (1816?–1875?), a native school teacher and in 1845 and 1846 a member of the Choctaw council, compiled and edited the volume. Carney was an old Choctaw Academy boy.

The slaveholding Choctaw were a perfectly realistic people: like other red emigrants from the oppressive jurisdiction of a white majority, they

[5] The name, probably an old war title, can not now be satisfactorily translated.

promptly devised laws, here printed, to insure the safe subordination of their own black minority.

DLC MH-L

The constitution, and laws of the Choctaw Nation. Printed at Doaksville, 1852. [111

110 p. 17.5 cm. Caption title.

Constitution adopted at Nanih Waiya October 14, 1850, and acts and resolutions of the regular October sessions annually from 1834 to 1850, inclusive, and of the regular session of November 1851, here numbered the 1st to 18th sessions. "Repealed laws are omitted; and amended laws are printed as amended."

The president of the constitutional convention at Nanih Waiya in 1850 was Peter Perkins Pitchlynn (1806–1881).

The volume was printed on the press of the *Choctaw Intelligencer*, a short-lived Doaksville weekly newspaper, in early 1852, about the time that it ceased publication or shortly afterward.

Doaksville, an important trading center and at the time the largest town in Indian Territory, lay in the southern part of the Choctaw Nation, a mile west of Fort Towson. Except for short periods of factional dispute it served as the capital of the Choctaw Nation from 1850 to 1863. Nothing remains of the town today but a few sticks and stones.

MH-L NNB OkTG

*Compilation, in Choctaw.* 1852.

Chahta yakni ikastitushvn micha i nan vlhpisa Tokosowil ak o atoba. 1852. [Doaksville, 1852.] [112

127 p. Caption title.

Not seen. Title and pagination are from Carolyn Thomas Foreman, *Oklahoma Imprints* (1936), 42. Mrs. Foreman tells me that the printing date 1842 given in her book is a misprint for 1852, and the latter date has accordingly been substituted in the title above. The copy which Mrs. Foreman recorded was one owned by the late Peter James Hudson, the Choctaw teacher, translator, and historian; unluckily, it can not now be found and no other is known.

The volume, a translation into Choctaw of the contents of the preceding volume, was printed on the *Intelligencer* press at Doaksville, the Tokosowil of the title. Like the English version, it had only a caption title.

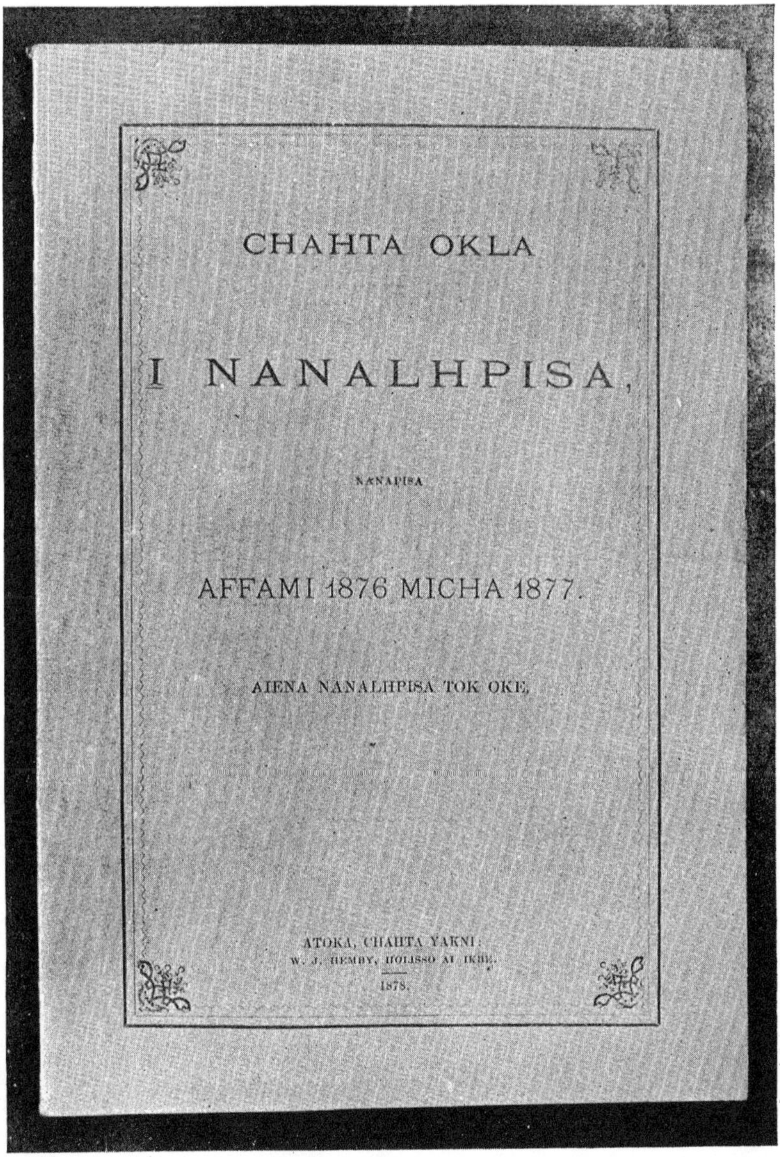

CHAHTA OKLA

I NANALHPISA,

NANAPISA

AFFAMI 1876 MICHA 1877.

AIENA NANALHPISA TOK OKE.

ATOKA, CHAHTA YAKNI:
W. J. HEMBY, HOLISSO AI IKBE.

1878.

Wrapper Title of No. 127

The Choctaw council on November 8, 1853, appropriated $172 "to pay Capt[s]. Noel Gardner and Joseph Dukes for ninety-one copies of [the] constitution and laws now on hand and eighty-one copies which they lost in the recent conflagration of houses in Doaksville." The books destroyed were probably copies of this volume and the preceding one. It is not known how many of either were printed.

District captains Noel Gardner (b. 1811?) and Joseph Dukes (1811–1861), each of whom had a son who became principal chief,[6] were Choctaw mixed bloods deeply interested in the advancement of their people and for many years interpreters and translators for the missionaries. It would appear from the appropriation act quoted in part above that they undertook on their own resources the publication of the two volumes. The translation into Choctaw may also have been their joint work. A translation by Dukes into Choctaw of portions of the Old Testament was published at Utica, New York, in 1831, just before the tribe left Mississippi. Dukes, who served for several years as official translator for the council, was one of the framers of the Doaksville constitution adopted in January 1860 and later the same year a candidate for the office of principal chief at the first election held under that constitution. Gardner when a boy attended the Choctaw Academy in Kentucky and was a member of the council in 1855.

The constitution of the Choctaw Nation, adopted January, 1857. Printed by Wheeler & Sparks, Herald Office, Fort Smith, Arkansas. 1857. [113

19 p. 20.5 cm.

The constitution was adopted in convention at Skullyville, an important Choctaw town, now deserted, 18 miles west of Fort Smith.

Tandy Walker (1814–1877), of Skullyville, one of the leaders of the "progressive" faction of the tribe, served as the president of the convention. In 1858 and 1859 he held the office of governor under this short-lived constitution and in the Civil War he commanded the 1st Choctaw and Chickasaw Mounted Rifles in the service of the Confederate States. Colonel Walker when a boy attended the Choctaw Academy in Kentucky.

The adoption of the Skullyville constitution, which substituted for the district chiefs and council a governor and legislature after the American plan, proved to be only a partial victory for the "progressives"; its

[6] Namely, Jefferson Gardner, principal chief 1894–1896, and Gilbert Wesley Dukes, principal chief 1900–1902.

force was never acknowledged by the conservative element of the tribe and it was superseded in 1860 by the compromise constitution adopted at Doaksville.

OkTG

**Acts and resolutions of the General Council of the Choctaw Nation, from 1852 to 1857, both inclusive. Published by authority of the General Council. Fort Smith, Ark. Josephus Dotson, printer for the Nation. 1858.** [114

240 p. 21 cm. Issued in boards and also in printed wrappers.

Constitution, treaty of 1855 between the United States and the Choctaw and Chickasaw, and acts and resolutions of the regular November sessions of 1852, 1853, 1854, and 1855, the extra session of July and the regular session of November 1856, and the regular session of October 1857. The regular sessions of November 1852 to November 1856, inclusive, are here numbered the 19th to 23rd. After adoption of the Skullyville constitution the serial numbering of sessions was abandoned.

The acts of October 1857 include a civil and criminal code.

The volume was printed by Wheeler & Sparks at the *Times* office for Josephus Dotson, at the time secretary of the Choctaw council but not himself a printer. Dotson, a native of Mississippi, practiced law intermittently at Fort Smith. He is said to have been the first white man to hold office in the Choctaw government.

DJ DLC M MiU-L MnU-L NNB OkTG OkU-P TxU

On November 4, 1857, the council authorized the governor "to have the acts and resolutions passed at the present session printed in pamphlet form both in English and Choctaw, if practicable, if not, in English alone, at as early a date as possible." Jonathan Edwards Dwight and Jacob Folsom, native Choctaw, were appointed translators. Again, on January 19, 1858, the council authorized the translation into Choctaw and the printing in an edition of 400 copies of "all laws passed from October 1857 to the close of the present session." The plan for a separate sessional volume seems, however, to have been abandoned in favor of the foregoing compilation.

Governor Tandy Walker in a letter to Peter Folsom dated April 26, 1858, wrote that he had just received from Josephus Dotson, secretary of the council, a printed copy of the compilation, the foregoing volume, and that he had sent it "to the translators for them to put it in Choctaw." On February 26, 1859, he wrote to Peter P. Pitchlynn,[7] "We are having the laws printed in Choctaw." If such a volume was actually printed, and it is doubtful that it was, no copy has survived. Nor, indeed, is the translation known today in manuscript.

Acts and resolutions of the General Council of the Choctaw Nation, at the called sessions thereof, held in April and June 1858, and the regular session held in October, 1858. Published by authority of the General Council. Fort Smith, Ark. Josephus Dotson, printer for the Nation. 1859. [115

80 p. 21 cm.

The following imprint appears on the verso of the title: Fort Smith: Wheeler & Sparks, printers. Washington Street, Garrison block, two doors from City Hotel.

Constitution, and the acts and resolutions described in the title.

**DLC ICLaw MH-L MiU-L MnU-L NNB OkHi OkTG**

Acts and resolutions of the General Council of the Choctaw Nation, for the year 1859. Published by authority of the General Council. Fort Smith, Ark. Printed at the Times Office for Campbell LeFlore, printer for the Choctaw Nation. 1860. [116

53, [1] p. 21.5 cm.

The constitution, and the acts and resolutions of the regular session of October 1859.

The volume was printed by Wheeler & Sparks.

Campbell LeFlore (1830–1896), a Choctaw mixed blood of French descent and a nephew of Principal Chief Basil LeFlore, was secretary of the Choctaw council; there is no evidence that he was himself a printer. LeFlore was elected to the council in 1863 and when the Confederate States district courts for Indian Territory were tardily organized in February 1865 he was appointed district attorney for the District of Tushka Homma. He later took up the practice of law at Fort Smith but continued to play an active part in Choctaw affairs. The LeFlore family was long one of the most prominent in the tribe.

**DLC ICLaw MnU-L NNB OkHi OkTG**

[7] The two letters by Governor Walker are in the Pitchlynn papers. See p. 55.

**Resolutions passed by the convention of the Choctaws and Chickasaws, held at Boggy Depot, March 11th, 1861. [Boggy Depot, 1861.]** [117

Broadside. 36 cm. 2 columns.

The resolutions, adopted March 16, contain a joint agreement, which came to nothing, to sectionize communal lands and allot them equally to all members of the two tribes.

The leaf was printed at the office of the *National Register.*

Tandy Walker (1814–1877), the mixed blood Choctaw already noticed as president of the Skullyville convention and as governor of the Choctaw Nation under the short-lived Skullyville constitution, served as president of the Choctaw and Chickasaw convention.

Boggy Depot, a trading center for Choctaw and Chickasaw Indians, lay about twenty-five miles below the convergence of the main road to Texas from the North and the Fort Smith road to the Southwest, or about eight miles southwest of the present Atoka. The village, which has all but disappeared, served as the Choctaw capital in 1858 and 1859, that is, for the life of the Skullyville constitution, and later was an important Confederate military post.

OkTG

**Constitution and laws of the Choctaw Nation. Boggy Depot, Choctaw Nation: 1861. Printed by J. Hort. Smith, proprietor of the National Register.** [118

137 p. 21 cm. Pages 39–119 are wrongly numbered 31–111.

The constitution adopted at Doaksville January 11, 1860, and the acts and resolutions of the regular session of October 1860 and the extra session of January 1861. The acts of October 1860 include a revised civil and criminal code. For an act omitted from this volume see No. 122 of this bibliography.

150 copies were ordered printed.

This is the only volume of Indian session laws now known to have been printed within the jurisdiction of the Confederate States of America. The Gilcrease Foundation owns a copy of the *National Register* (Vol. 1, No. 11, June 1, 1861), the sole example known to survive, in which the editor, J. Hort. Smith, advertised for "two practical printers to assist in printing the laws of the Choctaw Nation"—this volume. Printing was completed in July.

The president of the Doaksville convention was the mixed blood George Hudson (1808–1865), of Eagletown, who was later in the year elected principal chief.

The Doaksville constitution, which revived the old principal chieftainship in name, superseded the Skullyville constitution in force since 1857; with few amendments it met the needs of the Choctaw for the remainder of their tribal life.

The bibliographer owns, in the Pitchlynn papers, the unpublished manuscript originals, in English, of the acts and resolutions of this and several subsequent Confederate sessions of the Choctaw council.

OkTG

An act of the council passed October 18, 1862, provided for "the Constitution, Laws and Resolutions, and all other documents proper to be printed for the benefit of the Choctaw people to be embodied in one book with complete index." 500 copies each were to be printed in English and Choctaw. The project was found too ambitious for wartime and was soon abandoned.

Resolutions expressing the sentiments and feelings of the General Council of the Choctaw Nation in relation to the warriors of that Nation now in the service of their country. [Washington, Arkansas, 1864.] [119

Broadside. 24 cm.

The following imprint appears at the end: Washington Telegraph.

The resolution is dated October 10, 1864.

OkTG

Head Quarters, Dist. Ind. Ter'y. Fort Towson, C. N., Oct. 31st, 1864. The following act of the General Council of the Choctaw Nation is published for information. By order of Major Gen'l. Maxey. M. L. Bell, A. A. Gen'l. An act entitled an act requiring the District Chiefs of this Nation to employ or make arrangements with citizens to hire wagons to haul supplies for the indigent and Choctaw refugees. [Fort Towson, 1864.] [120

Broadside. 20.5 cm.

The act, passed at a regular session of the council at Chahta Tamaha, was approved October 13, 1864.

The leaf was printed on the Confederate army press at Fort Towson.

Chahta Tamaha (that is, Choctaw town), the seat of Armstrong Academy three and a half miles northeast of the present town of Bokchito, Oklahoma, was the capital of the Choctaw Nation from 1863 to 1883.

Fort Towson was established in 1824 for the protection of Choctaw Indians voluntarily emigrating from Mississippi. It lay on the east bank of Gates Creek, about six miles above the junction of the Kiamichi and Red rivers. Abandoned by the army in 1854, it served as the Choctaw capital during a factional dispute in 1855 and 1856 and it housed a United States Choctaw agency until 1857 when all the buildings there were destroyed by fire. Confederate forces occupied its strategic location for most of the Civil War period.

OkTG

Law regulating the granting of permits to trade, in the Choctaw Nation. [Fort Smith, 1868.] [121

3, [1] p. 22 cm. Caption title.

The last page is devoted to an advertisement of the Fort Smith Herald Book and Job Printing Establishment, the printers of the leaf.

The act was approved November 20, 1867. A printed certificate of authenticity at the end is dated December 4, 1868.

OkTG Wright

Constitution and laws of the Choctaw Nation. Together with the treaties of 1855, 1865 and 1866. Published by authority and direction of the General Council by Joseph P. Folsom, commissioned for the purpose, Chahta Tamaha, 1869. Wm. P. Lyon & Son, printers and publishers, New York City. [1869.] [122

508 p. 22 cm.

The constitution, and amendments of 1862, laws in force, and the 1855 and 1866 treaties with the United States. There was no treaty of 1865.

On p. 334 appears an act of October 31, 1860, which was omitted from the sessional issue (No. 118 of this bibliography) printed at Boggy Depot in 1861.

The volume was commonly known, from the initials of its compiler, as the J. P. code.

Joseph Pitchlynn Folsom (1823–1889) was a lawyer who had been educated at tribal expense at the Choctaw Academy and at Dartmouth

College. He served at various times as delegate to the Okmulgee council, member of the Choctaw council and president of the senate and was once a candidate for the office of principal chief. Folsom, who had three-fourths Choctaw blood, married a woman of the Seneca tribe.

Laws of the Choctaw Nation, relating to schools and scholars. Published by authority. Fort Smith, Ark.: printed by John F. Wheeler, at the Herald Office. 1869. [123

8 p. 21.5 cm. Wrapper title.

School laws in force. The dates of passage do not appear.

DNA

Charter of the Choctaw and Chickasaw Thirty-fifth Parallel Railroad Company. Published by the company, for the information of the Choctaw and Chickasaw peoples. Chahta Chikasha itatuklo chata palelil pokole tuchena akocha tulhape bachaya ka tuli hina kumpeni oke. Chahta mikmut Chikasha okla nana akostanecha chi pulla kuk o kumpeni illuput holisso ha ikbe tok oke. Little Rock, Ark.: Woodruff & Blocher, printers, binders and stationers, Markham Street. 1870. [124

[5], 24 (in double numbers) p. 26.5 cm. Printed wrappers. Text in English and in Choctaw, the two versions on alternate pages facing each other.

The title above is the wrapper title. The regular title reads as follows: Charter of the Choctaw and Chickasaw Thirty-fifth Parallel Railroad Company, passed by the General Council of the Choctaw Nation, and approved April 8th, 1870. Chahta Chikasha itatuklo chata palelil pokole tuchena akocha tulhape bachaya ka tuli hina kumpeni oke.

This act and the following one were adopted at a special session in April and repealed at the regular session of October 1870, the railroad project having been disapproved at Washington.

James Margarum Pomeroy (1838–1887), of Little Rock, who was the attorney for the company, edited the volume and wrote the marginal notes. Pomeroy prepared the official edition of the debates and proceedings of the Arkansas constitutional convention of 1868 and published annotations of the Arkansas constitutions of 1868 and 1874. He was a native of New Jersey.

John Page (1820–1873), a native Choctaw long interpreter and translator for the missionaries, the Indian agents, and the Choctaw council, and an itinerant Methodist preacher to the full bloods, made the translation, an official one, into Choctaw. Page, who probably derived his English name and his denominational affiliation from the pioneer Mississippi Methodist circuit rider, attended the Choctaw Academy in his youth. He served as delegate to the Skullyville constitutional convention in 1857, as member of the council in 1861, as district judge in 1863, and as delegate to Washington and treaty commissioner in 1866. In the Civil War he was a major in Colonel Jackson McCurtain's 3rd Choctaw Regiment. Partly, perhaps, because of his increasing preoccupation with temporal affairs but chiefly because of a sudden, unorthodox addiction to strong drink of all kinds, Page was unfrocked by a sorrowing Methodist conference in 1867.

OkTG

**Charter of the Choctaw and Chickasaw Central Railroad Company. Published for the information of the Choctaw and Chickasaw peoples. Chahta Chikasha itatuklo chata iklvna tvli hina kvmpeni oke. Chahta mikmvt Chikasha okla nana akostenecha chi pulla kuk o holisso illvpvt toba hoke. Little Rock, Ark.: Woodruff and Blocher, printers, binders and stationers, Markham Street. 1870.** [125

v, 24 (in double numbers) p. Text in English and in Choctaw, on alternate pages facing each other.

Not seen. Title and collation are from James Constantine Pilling, *Bibliography of the Muskhogean Languages* (1889), 71. Pilling, whose information about the volume was itself second-hand, did not see a copy, and none has been found by the present bibliographer.

James Margarum Pomeroy (1838–1887) edited the volume and John Page (1820–1873) made the translation into Choctaw.

**Laws of the Choctaw Nation passed at the Choctaw councils of 1876 and 1877. Atoka, Choctaw Nation: W. J. Hemby, printer. 1878.** [126

71 p. 22 cm. Printed wrappers.

Acts and resolutions of the extra session of March 1876 and the regular October sessions of 1876 and 1877.

250 copies were ordered printed.

W. J. Hemby, a white man, was at various times between 1872 and 1878 the editor, printer, or proprietor of newspapers at the Choctaw towns of New Boggy, Atoka, and Caddo.

*Acts of 1876 and 1877, in Choctaw.* 1878.

Chahta okla i nanalhpisa, nanapisa affami 1876 micha 1877. Aiena nanalhpisa tok oke. Atoka, Chahta yakni: W. J. Hemby, holisso ai ikbe. 1878. [127

61 p. 22 cm. Printed wrappers.

The contents of the preceding volume, translated into Choctaw, probably by Allen Wright (1826–1885), already noticed as the compiler and translator of No. 95 of this bibliography.

The volume was printed at Atoka by W. J. Hemby. 250 copies were ordered printed.

M MH-L OkHi OkTG OkU-P

Acts and resolutions passed at the regular term of the General Council of the Choctaw Nation. October, 1880. From Nos. 1 to 41 inclusive. Denison, Texas: M. F. Dearing, lessee Herald Job Office, printer. 1880. [128

29 p. 21 cm. Wrapper title.

The contents are fully described in the title.

ICN NNB OkHi OkTG OkU-P

General and special laws of the Choctaw Nation, passed at the regular session of the General Council, convened at Chahta Tamaha, October 3rd and adjourned November 12th, 1881. By authority. Denison, Texas: The "News" Job Printing House, Murray & Dearing, 1881. [129

66 p. 21.5 cm. Printed wrappers.

Acts and resolutions described in the title and a financial statement.

MH-L NNB OkHi OkTG

*Acts of 1881, in Choctaw.* 1881.

Chahta okla i nanalhpisa, nanapesa affammi 1881 chiiya ka. Ahlopulli tok. Chahta anompa atoshoa. Tanisin, Teksis, Murray & Dearing, holisso ai ikbe. 1881. [Denison, Texas.] [130

44 p. 21 cm. Printed wrappers.

The contents of the preceding volume, the financial statement omitted, translated into Choctaw.

CtY OkHi

General and special laws of the Choctaw Nation, passed at the regular session of the General Council, convened at Chahta Tamaha. October 2nd, and adjourned November 4th 1882. By authority. Denison, Texas: The "News" Job Printing House, Murray & Dearing. 1881 [*for* 1882]. [131

38 p. 21 cm. Printed wrappers.

Acts and resolutions described in the title and a financial statement.

MoSL NNB OkHi OkTG

*Acts of* 1882, *in Choctaw*. 1882.

Chahta okla i nanalhpisa, nanapesa affammi 1882 chiiya ka. Ahlopulli tok. Chahta anompa atoshoa. Tanisin, Teksis: Murray & Dearing, holisso ai ikbe. 1882. [Denison, Texas.] [132

42 p. 22 cm. Printed wrappers.

The contents of the preceding volume, the financial statement omitted, translated into Choctaw.

MH-L OkHi

The freedmen and registration bills, passed at a special session of the Choctaw Council, Indian Territory. May, 1883. Denison, Texas. Printed at Murray's Steam Printing House. 1883. [133

8 p. 22 cm. Wrapper title.

Two acts approved May 21.

MH-L OkTG

Laws of the Choctaw Nation, passed at the Choctaw Council at the regular session of 1883. Sedalia, Mo.: Democrat Steam Printing House and Book Bindery. 1883. [134

71, [1] p. 22.5 cm. Printed wrappers.

C DJ ICLaw ICN MH-L OkHi OkTG T

*Acts of* 1883, *in Choctaw*. 1883.

Chahta okla i nan ulhpesa. Nan apis a ittafama he aiahlpiesa afammi, 1883. Chiiyah mut ahlopulli chi tuk. Democrat oka wahlalli talli aiisht i chuli micha holisso hakshop asha aiikbi Sitilia, Mo. 1883. [Sedalia, Missouri.] [135

87 p. 22 cm. Printed wrappers.

The contents of the preceding volume, the index omitted, translated into Choctaw.

The volume was printed at the Democrat Steam Printing House and Book Bindery.

MH-L OkHi

General and special laws of the Choctaw Nation passed at the regular session of the General Council convened at Tushka Homma, October 6 and adjourned November 7. By authority. Muskogee: Indian Journal Steam Job print, 1884. [136

47 p. 21 cm. Printed wrappers.

Acts and resolutions of the regular session of October 1884.

Tushka Homma became the permanent capital of the Choctaw Nation in 1883. The village lay about two miles north of the present Tuskahoma, Oklahoma, and about two and a half miles northeast of Nanih Waiya, the first Choctaw capital in the West.

ICN NNB OkHi OkTG

*Acts of* 1884, *in Choctaw.* 1885.

Chahta okla i nan ahlpesa, Tashka Homma ya, Aktoba 1884. Nan apesa chiiya ma ahlopulli tok, Chahta imanompa. Muskogee, I. T.: Oka wahlalli tali isht ai i chuli, 1885. [137

54 p. 22.5 cm. Printed wrappers.

The contents of the preceding volume, translated into Choctaw.

The volume was printed at the *Indian Journal* office.

ICN OkHi OkTG

Laws of the Choctaw Nation, passed at the Choctaw Council at the regular session of 1886. Sedalia, Mo. Democrat Publishing Company, steam printers and binders. 1886. [138

53 p. 22 cm. Printed wrappers.

Acts and resolutions of the regular session of October 1886.

DJ DLC OkHi OkTG

*Acts of 1886, in Choctaw.* 1887.

Chahta okla i nanulhpisa, nanapesa afafmmi 1886 chiiya ka. Ahlopulli tok. Chahta anumpa atoshoa. Sedalia, Mo. Democrat Publishing Company, 1887. [139

49, [1], iii p. 21.5 cm. Printed wrappers.

The contents of the preceding volume, translated into Choctaw.

DLC MH-L OkHi OkTG

Constitution, treaties and laws of the Choctaw Nation. Made and enacted by the Choctaw Legislature. 1887. Democrat Steam print, Sedalia, Mo. [140

200, iv p. 22.5 cm.

Variant 1: The Gilcrease Foundation has a copy with the following paging after p. 10: 11/16, 17/14, 15/12, 13/18. Paging is wrong; the text is regular and uninterrupted.

Variant 2: The Gilcrease Foundation has another copy with the following paging after p. 50: 55/52, 53/58, 51/56, 57/54. Page numbers are right but the forms were wrongly arranged for printing and the text is consequently disordered.

The constitution and an amendment of 1883, revised statutes, and treaties with the United States of 1837, 1855, and 1866.

Commonly known as the Standley code, the volume was compiled by James Stirman Standley (1841–1904), of Atoka, a lawyer and newspaper publisher. A latecomer (1873) from Mississippi, Standley had little Choctaw blood but enough to establish tribal citizenship.

CtY-L DIA DLC Ia-L M MH-L N-L NN OkTG

*Revised statutes, in Choctaw.* 1887.

Chahta okla i kanstitioshun, choleti micha nan ulhpisa aiena. Chahta okla i nan apesa yut apesa tok mak oke. Sedalia, Mo., Democrat Publishing Company. 1887. [141

235 p. 22 cm.

The contents of the preceding volume, translated into Choctaw.

NN OkHi OkTG

Acts and resolutions of the Choctaw Council for the year 1887. Phoenix Steam print, Muskogee, I. T. 1888. [142

31 p. 21 cm. Printed wrappers.

Acts and resolutions of the regular session of October 1887.

DJ ICLaw NNB OkHi OkTG

Acts and resolutions of the Choctaw Council. For the year 1888. Muskogee, Ind. Ter. The Phoenix Printing Company. Steam book and job printers. 1888. [143

39, [2] p. 21 cm. Printed wrappers.

Acts and resolutions of the regular session of October 1888.

DJ DLC ICLaw MiU-L NNB OkHi OkTG

Laws of the Choctaw Nation passed at the regular session of the General Council convened at Tushka Humma, October 7th, 1889, and adjourned November 15, 1889. Atoka, Ind. Ter. Indian Citizen Publishing Co. 1890. [144

60, [1] p. 22.5 cm. Printed wrappers.

Acts and resolutions of the regular session of October and the extra session of December 1889.

DJ DLC DNA ICLaw In-SC MH-L OkHi OkTG

Laws of the Choctaw Nation passed at the regular session of the General Council convened at Tushka Humma October 6, 1890, adjourned November 14, 1890. [Paris, Texas, 1890.] [145

44 p. 22.5 cm. Printed wrappers.

The following imprint appears on the verso of the title: Marshall's Printing House, Paris, Texas.

The contents are fully described in the title.

DJ OkHi OkTG

Laws of the Choctaw Nation passed at the regular session of the General Council convened at Tushka Humma October 6, 1890, adjourned November 14, 1890. [Paris, Texas, 1890.] [146

43 p. 22.5 cm. Printed wrappers.

The following imprint appears on the verso of the title: Marshall's Printing House, Paris, Texas.

This and the preceding volume have identical contents. There is internal evidence to establish the order of their printing but nothing to show why it became necessary to reset the type and print a second edition.

ICLaw MH-L OkTG

Laws of the Choctaw Nation made and enacted by the General Council, from 1886 to 1890 inclusive. 1890. Indian Citizen print, Atoka, I. T. [147

[2], 53, [2], 62 p. 22.5 cm. Text in English and in Choctaw.

A selection of laws in force.

The cover wrongly states that the volume contains laws from 1886 to 1891, inclusive.

250 copies were ordered printed.

ICLaw KHi MH-L MnU-L NNB OkHi OkTG

Laws of the Choctaw Nation made and enacted by the General Council, from 1886 to 1890 inclusive. 1891. Indian Citizen print, Atoka, I. T. [148

But for the printing date on the title-page this volume is identical in every particular with the preceding one.

An act relating to the school system of the Choctaw Nation. Approved October 31, 1890. Atoka, I. T.: printed at the Indian Citizen Office. 1891. [149

14 p. 22.5 cm. Printed wrappers. A slip bearing an amendment of December 13, 1891, is pasted down on the verso of the title.

MnU-L OkHi

Laws of the Choctaw Nation passed at the special session of the General Council convened at Tushka Humma April 6, 1891, and adjourned April 11, 1891. [Paris, Texas, 1891.] [150

19 p. 22.5 cm. Wrapper title.

The contents are fully described in the title.

The volume was printed at Marshall's Printing House.

DJ DLC ICLaw MH-L MiU-L MnU-L OkHi OkTG

Whereas the Congress of the United States did on the 3rd day of March A. D. 1891, make an appropriation of the sum of $2,991,450 in favor of the Choctaw and Chickasaw nations of Indians, for their right, title and interest in certain lands west of 98° west longitude, and now occupied by the Cheyenne, and Arapahoe tribes of Indians. [Talihina? 1891.] [151

Broadside. 22 cm. 2 columns. Printed without caption; the title above is the first paragraph of the text.

The act, approved by the principal chief October 19, 1891, voided certain contracts with attorneys and provided for a special tribal delegation to visit Washington.

The place of printing is conjectured from the circumstance that the *Talihina Signal* at this time had the printing press closest to Tuskha Homma, the Choctaw capital.

**DNA**

**Laws of the Choctaw Nation** passed at the regular session of the General Council convened at Tushka Humma, 1891. [Paris, Texas, 1892.] [152

47 p. 22.5 cm. Printed wrappers.

The following imprint appears on the verso of the title: Marshall's Printing House, Paris, Texas.

Acts and resolutions of the regular session of October and the extra session of December 1891.

**DLC MH-L OkHi OkTG**

**Laws of the Choctaw Nation** passed at the regular session of the General Council convened at Tushka Humma October 3rd, 1992 [*for* 1892], and adjourned November 4th, 1892. Atoka, Ind. Ter. Indian Citizen Publishing Co. 1893. [153

24, ii p. 21.5 cm. Printed wrappers.

The contents are fully described in the title.

**DLC MH-L MnU-L OkHi OkTG**

**Laws of the Choctaw Nation** passed at the regular session of the General Council convened at Tushka Homma, Oct. 2, 1893, and adjourned Oct. 27, 1893, and the special sessions convened in February 1892, [*for* 1893] and convened in June, 1893. Atoka, Ind. Ter. Indian Citizen Publishing Co. 1894. [154

[1], 40, [2] p. 20.5 cm. Printed wrappers.

The contents are fully described in the title.

**MH-L NNB OkHi OkTG**

Constitution and laws of the Choctaw Nation. Together with the treaties of 1837, 1855, 1865 and 1866. Published by authority of the General Council by A. R. Durant, commissioned for the purpose, and Davis Homer and Ben Watkins, assistant compilers. Dallas, Texas: John F. Worley, printer and publisher, 1894. [155

352 p. 22 cm. A leaf of two unnumbered pages is inserted between p. 314 and p. 315.

The constitution and amendments, a revision of the statutes approved October 30, 1888, and subsequent amendments, and acts in force of the extra session of May 1883, the regular October sessions of 1886, 1887, 1888, 1889, and 1890, the extra session of April, the regular session of October, and the extra session of December 1891, and the extra session of June and the regular session of October 1893; the United States patent to Choctaw lands, and the treaties with the United States of 1837, 1855, and 1866. There was no treaty of 1865.

Although it had a wide practical use, the Durant code, as this volume was commonly known, was never officially approved; it lacked the dates of passage of most of the laws, and the council is said to have refused in consequence to pay for its printing. 500 copies were ordered printed.

Alexander Richard Durant (b. 1839), a Choctaw lawyer and sometime Presbyterian preacher, was at various times speaker of the lower house of the Choctaw council, journalist of the senate, national secretary, attorney general, supreme judge, national delegate, and a candidate for the office of principal chief. He served for a time as interpreter for the United States district court at Paris, Texas. Judge Durant was born in the old Choctaw Nation in Mississippi.

Ben Watkins, a native of Virginia and a Choctaw citizen by marriage, was an influential lawyer and school teacher and at one time the private secretary of Principal Chief Wilson N. Jones. He compiled a Choctaw definer printed at Van Buren, Arkansas, in 1892.

Davis Aaron Homer or Homma (b. 1864?), a full blood Choctaw, has already been noticed as the compiler of No. 105 of this bibliography and the translator of No. 106.

*Revised statutes, in Choctaw.* 1894.

Chahta oklah i nanvlhpisa noshkobo micha nanvlhpisa. Mikmut afammih 1837, 1855, 1865, 1866 kash nanitimapisa tok (treaties) aiena ho Chahta oklah i nanupisa chito ut upisa toko anotaka hosh

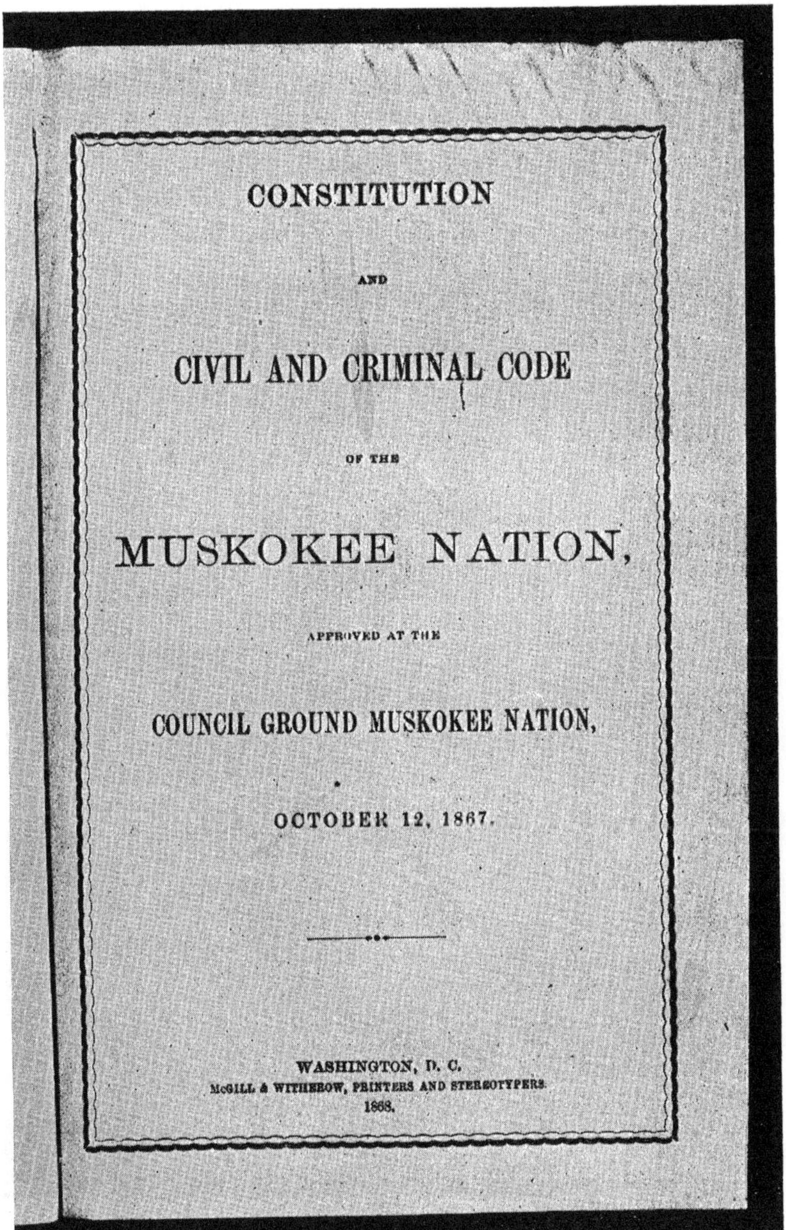

CONSTITUTION

AND

CIVIL AND CRIMINAL CODE

OF THE

MUSKOKEE NATION,

APPROVED AT THE

COUNCIL GROUND MUSKOKEE NATION,

OCTOBER 12, 1867.

WASHINGTON, D. C.
McGILL & WITHEROW, PRINTERS AND STEREOTYPERS.
1868.

Wrapper Title of No. 169

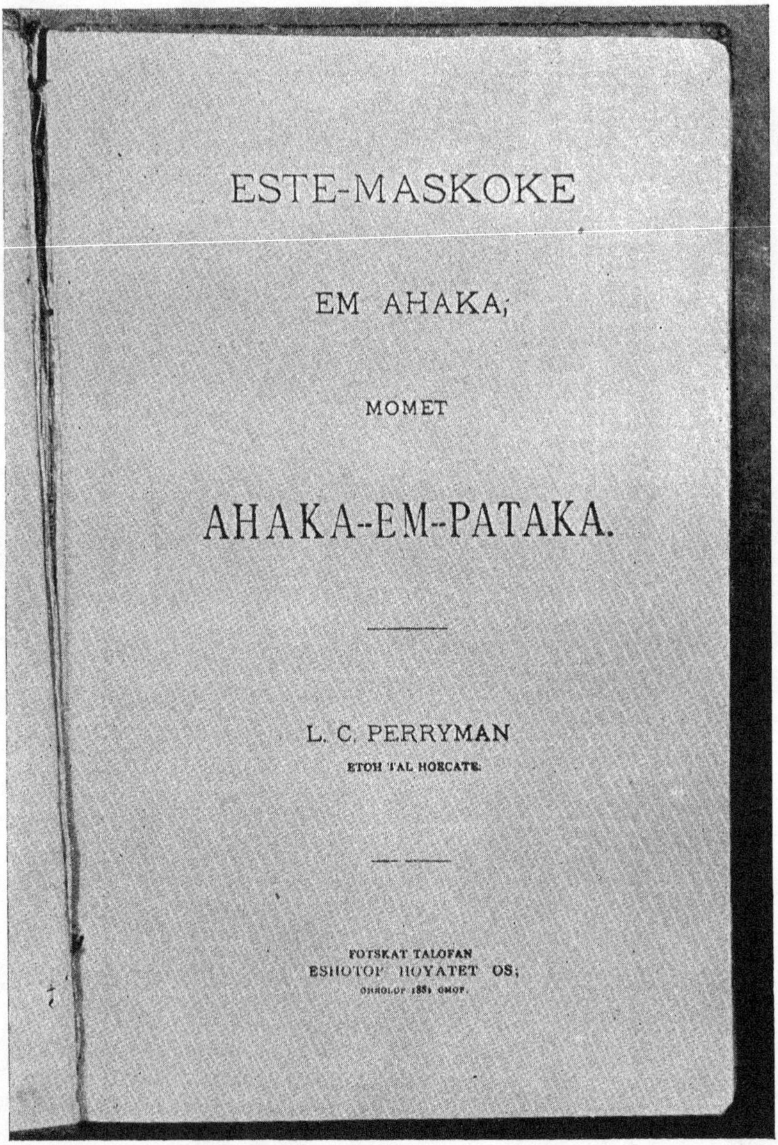

ESTE-MASKOKE

EM AHAKA;

MOMET

AHAKA--EM-PATAKA.

L. C. PERRYMAN

ETOH TAL HOECATE.

FOTSKAT TALOFAN

ESHOTOF HOYATET OS;

OHHOLOF 188[illegible] OMOF.

Title Page of No. 172

A. R. Durant, ut ulhtuka yosh holisso achafa ilapa foki hoke. Davis Homer micha Ben Watkins, apiluchi. John F. Worley, holisso tulli isht ichuli micha holisso ikbi Tullis, Teksis. 1894. [Dallas, Texas.] [156

428 p. 22 cm.

The contents of the preceding volume, translated into Choctaw by Davis A. Homer and Ben Watkins, the assistant compilers.

The Choctaw laws. Passed at the special sessions in January, 1894, and April, 1894, and the regular session, October, 1894. National Advocate print, Antlers, I. T. [1895.] [157

[2], 44 p. 22 cm. Printed wrappers.

A copy has been seen with the verso of p. 43 blank; it is misprinted and incomplete.

The contents are fully described in the title.

**MH-L MnU-L NNB OkHi OkTG**

Acts of Council of the Choctaw Nation, passed at the regular sessions of October 1895 and 1896, and the special session of September, 1896. Choctaw News, Talihina, I. T. [1897.] [158

108, [2] p. 21 cm. Printed wrappers.

The contents are fully described in the title.

**DJ NNB OkHi OkTG PPB**

Acts and resolutions of the General Council of the Choctaw Nation, passed at its regular session, October, 1897; and also all the school laws of the Choctaw Nation. Elevator Job Office, December, 1897. [Fort Smith.] [159

66 p. 21.5 cm. Printed wrappers.

Acts and resolutions of the regular session of October 1897 and the school law of October 31, 1890.

**DLC ICLaw M MH-L MnU-L NNB OkHi OkTG PPB**

Acts and resolutions of the General Council of the Choctaw Nation passed at its regular session, 1898, and its special session, 1899. Caddo, Ind. Ter., The Herald Press, 1899. [160

[2], 69 p. 21 cm. Printed wrappers.

Acts and resolutions of the regular session of October 1898 and the extra session of March 1899.

**DIA DJ DLC M MH-L NNB OkHi OkTG PPB**

Acts and resolutions of the General Council of the Choctaw Nation. Passed at its regular session 1899. News Press, South M'Alester, 1900. [161

71, [2] p. 21.5 cm. Wrapper title.

Acts and resolutions of the regular session of October 1899.

**DLC MH-L MnU-L OkHi OkTG**

Acts and resolutions of the General Council of the Choctaw Nation passed at its regular session, 1900, and extra session, 1901. Herald Press, Caddo. 1901. [162

57 p. 21.5 cm. Wrapper title.

Acts and resolutions of the regular session of October 1900 and the extra session of January 1901.

**DLC OkHi OkTG**

Acts and resolutions of the General Council of the Choctaw Nation passed at its regular session, 1901. Herald Press, Caddo. 1902.

42, [2] p. 21 cm. Wrapper title. [163

Acts and resolutions of the regular session of October 1901.

**DLC MH-L OkHi OkTG**

Acts and resolutions of the General Council of the Choctaw Nation, passed at its regular session, 1902, and extra session, 1902. Husonian Press, Hugo, 1903. [164

85 p. 21.5 cm. A printed slip bearing a one-line correction is pasted down on p. 73.

Acts and resolutions of the regular session of October and the extra session of December 1902.

Ordinances of the Town of Wilburton, Ind. Ter. Incorporated June 24, 1902. Wilburton, Ind. Ter. The News print. 1903. [165

38 p. 21.5 cm. Wrapper title. The inside of the back wrapper bears a list of the town officers.

Ordinances passed by the mayor and council from August 27, 1902, to April 21, 1903.

The present Wilburton, Oklahoma, formerly lay in the Choctaw Nation.

**OkTG**

Acts and resolutions of the General Council of the Choctaw Nation passed at its regular session, 1903. Hugo Husonian job print. [Hugo, 1904.] [166

63 p. 21 cm. Wrapper title. An errata slip is inserted at the front.

Acts and resolutions of the regular session of October 1903.

**DLC MH-L MiU-L NN NNB OkHi OkMu OkTG OkU**

Acts and resolutions of the General Council, of the Choctaw Nation. Passed at its regular session, 1904. Hugo Husonian, steam job print. [Hugo, 1905.] [167

48 p. 21.5 cm. Wrapper title.

Acts and resolutions of the regular session of October 1904.

**DLC MH-L MiU-L MnU-L NNB OkHi OkMu OkTG OkU**

Acts and resolutions of the General Council of the Choctaw Nation. Passed at its extraordinary and regular sessions, 1905. [Hugo? 1906.] [168

15, 56, [1] p. 20.5 cm. Wrapper title.

Acts and resolutions of the extra session of June and the regular session of October 1905.

**DLC MH-L OkHi OkTG**

# THE CREEK (OR MUSKOGEE) NATION

The Creek Indians, a confederacy forming the largest division of the Muskhogean family, formerly held most of present Georgia and Alabama and were first visited in 1540 by Hernando de Soto. In early times they were allied with the southern colonists against the Florida Spaniards, by whom they had been maltreated, and they sided with the British in the American Revolution and again in the War of 1812. Defeated in the so-called Creek War of 1813 and 1814, they were stripped of most of their lands and after another uprising in 1836, into which they had been goaded by increasingly covetous white neighbors, they were swiftly booted with their negroes to the West. At the outbreak of the Civil War slaveholders and southern sympathizers of their number committed the Creeks to an alliance with the Confederate States of America but the people themselves remained bitterly divided over the issues of the struggle and the alliance proved a ruinous one. Comprising one of the so-called Five Civilized Tribes, the Creeks became citizens of the United States in 1906 when their own government was dissolved. Their most famous man was the mixed blood Alexander McGillivray (1759?–1793) who became virtually a dictator by force of his ability to play off the English, French, and Spaniards against one another to the benefit of the Creeks.

The Creeks had ancient and highly organized separate town governments but under the persuasive leadership of Benjamin Hawkins (1754–1816), a United States Indian agent whom they named in their language Beloved Man of the Four Nations, they began in a small way in 1799 to accept imported ideas of centralized government, the first such step known to have been taken by any Indians of the present United States. Of this beginning

Hawkins himself in his "Sketch of the Creek Country in 1798 and 99" wrote the following:

> At a meeting of the national council, convened by order of the agent for Indian affairs, at Tookaubatche,[1] the 27th November, 1799, the chiefs, after a long and solemn deliberation, on the affairs of the nation, which were laid before them by the agent for Indian affairs, came to a resolution to adopt the plan of the agent, "to class all the towns, and to appoint a warrior over each class, denominated the warrior of the nation." [2]

Again, in greater detail, Hawkins wrote:

> The Creeks never had, till this year [1799], a national government and law. Everything of a general tendency, was left to the care and management of the public agents, who heretofore used temporary expedients only; and amongst the most powerful and persuasive, was the pressure of fear from without, and presents. The attempt, in the course of the last and present year, to establish a national council, to meet annually, and to make general regulations for the welfare of the nation, promises to succeed. The law passed at the first meeting, to punish thieves and mischief-makers, has been carried into effect, in a few instances, where the personal influence of the agent for Indian affairs, was greatly exerted. On a trying occasion, the chiefs were called on to turn out the warriors, and to punish the leaders of the banditti, who insulted the commissioners of Spain and the United States, on the 17th of September. After this was repeatedly urged, and the agent agreed to be responsible for all the consequences, the chiefs turned out the warriors and executed the law on the leader[3]

[1] An upper Creek town and an important tribal center which lay in a bend of the Tallapoosa River, on the west bank, two and a half miles below the present Tallassee, in Elmore County, Alabama. A tablet has been set up there to mark the spot.

[2] *Georgia Historical Society Collections,* III (1848), 51.

[3] A reference to William Augustus Bowles (1763–1805), a restless adventurer from Maryland and a former Tory, who managed several times to gain in the commercial interest of the British and with their aid enough of a malcontent following among the Lower Creeks in Florida to give McGillivray and the American and Spanish authorities some alarm. Bowles set up about this time the ambitious but artificial and evanescent State of Muskogee whose surviving official literature apparently consists of two flamboyant proclamations which he issued as Director General, a title which he had conferred with characteristic modesty upon himself. The earlier of the two, given out October 31, 1799, at headquarters at Wekina (Waukeenah), ordered United States and Spanish agents out of the State of Muskogee under threat of arrest. The bibliographer owns the unpublished

and a few of his associates, in an exemplary manner. While this transaction was fresh in the minds of the Indians, the agent for Indian affairs convened the national council, and made a report on the state of the nation to them, accompanied with his opinion of the plan indispensably necessary, to carry the laws of the nation into effect.

The council, after mature deliberation, determined that the safety of the nation was at stake; that having a firm reliance on the justice of the President of the United States, and the friendly attention of his agent for Indian affairs, they would adopt his plan.

1st. To class the towns, and appoint a warrior over each class, denominated the warrior of the nation, to superintend the execution of the law.

2d. To declare as law, that when a man is punished by the law of the nation, and dies, that it is the law that killed him. It is the nation who killed him; and that no man or family is to be held accountable for this act of the nation.

3d. That all mischief-makers and thieves, of any country of white people, shall be under the government of the agent for Indian affairs, and that he may introduce the troops of the United States to any part of the Creek country, to punish such persons; and that, when he calls in the troops of the United States, he is to call for such number of warriors as he may deem proper, to accompany them, to be under pay; that, in apprehending or punishing any white person, if Indians should interpose, the red warriors are to order them to desist; and if they refuse, the agent may order them to fire, at the same time ordering the troops of the United States to make common cause.[4]

In 1817 a formal law against murder was passed by the Creek council and reduced to writing by General William McIntosh (1755–1825), one of their chiefs. In 1819 another was passed by the council imposing penalties upon any clan returned to the

---

manuscript original, which is in General Bowles' own hand. The later one, issued February 1, 1802, at headquarters at Mekkessoky (Miccosukee), commissioned a privateer to harass Spanish shipping, war against Spain having been declared April 5, 1800, "by the Director General with the advice and consent of the Supreme Council of Muskogee." The manuscript original of the latter was in the possession some years ago of the late Wymberly Jones DeRenne, of Savannah, Georgia. It is unlikely that the State of Muskogee had written laws. At all events, if their contemporaries are to be credited, General Bowles' bizarre retinue did pretty well spontaneously at carousing and marauding without the extra urge immemorially supplied by legal prohibitions.

[4] *Georgia Historical Society Collections,* III (1848), 67.

nation after a sojourn in territory of a foreign tribe. These two laws, with the dates of their original passage, were included in a civil and criminal code adopted August 10, 1826, at Broken Arrow, a Lower Creek town on the Alabama side of the Chattahoochee River, a short distance from the present Columbus, Georgia. This document is not known to survive but the bibliographer owns an unpublished abstract of it made by Major, later Major General, Ethan Allen Hitchcock (1798–1870) while he was on a tour of investigation in Indian Territory in 1842.[5] The Hitchcock manuscript itself contains the 1817 law only in brief but that of 1819 and a number of those adopted in 1826 were copied in full. While he was about it, Major Hitchcock abstracted a body of laws "revised by a general council of the 18th of May, 1841," possibly the earliest adopted by the Creeks after their arrival in the West. The original tribal records, in English, were in the care in 1842 of James L. Alexander, a white trader and one of two clerks employed by the Creek Nation.

The earliest written laws of the Creeks were enacted and administered by chiefs, headmen, and lawyers or lawmakers. Under a constitution adopted about 1859 executive authority was held by four district principal chiefs elected "by the People or Voice of the Office Holders that may be present" and legislative authority by a general council whose members were presumably elected by the people. A new constitution adopted a year later but in the turmoil of the times probably never put into actual operation vested executive authority in a principal chief elected by the people and legislative authority in a council, composed of a committee and a house of warriors, whose members were similarly chosen. The 1867 constitution, which remained in force until the Creek government came to an end in 1906, vested executive authority in a principal chief elected by the people, legislative authority in a council composed of a house of kings and a house of warriors, both

[5] The abstract fills one of about a hundred original manuscript volumes of General Hitchcock's private journals, a portion of the papers withdrawn by his heirs in 1938 from deposit in the Library of Congress and sold by them to the bibliographer. These important journals have been published only in part and the volume containing the Creek laws is one of several entirely overlooked by investigators.

elected by the people, and judicial authority in a supreme court whose members were elected by the council.

Constitution and civil and criminal code of the Muskokee Nation, approved at the council ground Muskokee Nation, October 12, 1867. Washington, D. C. McGill & Witherow, printers and stereotypers. 1868. [169

15 p. 22.5 cm. Printed wrappers.

The constitution, which met the needs of the Creeks for the remainder of their tribal history, was adopted by a convention of the people at Black Jack Grove, on the south side of the Deep Fork River. Tribal meetings had formerly been held at High Spring, near Council Hill, about twenty miles east of Okmulgee. In 1868 Okmulgee was made the permanent capital.

The president of the convention was the full blood Samuel Checote (1819–1884), a Methodist preacher and the first principal chief elected under the new constitution. Checote had been one of the chiefs of the Confederate Creeks and had served in the Confederate army as a lieutenant colonel in command of Creek troops. He was born near Columbus, Georgia, in the old nation, and was a pupil in 1829 at the school established some years earlier near Fort Mitchell, Alabama, by the Reverend William Capers, the first Methodist missionary to the Creeks.

The texts of two earlier Creek constitutions, not dated, but adopted probably in 1859 and 1860, respectively, were preserved in a manuscript volume marked "Record Book of Chief Sam Checote in Early Sixties," the original of which the bibliographer has not located but of which the Oklahoma Historical Society has a typewritten copy. The volume contained also a civil and criminal code adopted at some time in the 1850's and many acts, but few of them dated, passed by the council in the fifties and sixties.

DLC OkTG

Constitution and laws of the Muskokee or Creek Nation, translated into Muskokee language, by S. W. & L. C. Perryman, by an act of the National Council. Washington City: McGill & Witherow, printers and stereotypers. 1868. [170

16 p. 22 cm. Printed wrappers.

The contents of the preceding volume, translated into Creek.

Sanford Ward Perryman (1834–1876) and Legus Chouteau Perryman (1838–1922), half-brothers, were members of an old and influential Creek family of mixed blood. The latter was principal chief from 1887 to 1895.

OkTG

Constitution and laws of the Muskogee Nation. Published by authority of the National Council. Saint Louis: Levison & Blythe Stationery Co., printers. 1880. [171

142 p. 22 cm.

The constitution, and the civil and criminal code of 1867 with amendments and additions; compiled statutes with amendments, and selected laws in force; United States statutes affecting Creek citizens; the compact of June 1870 with the Cherokee, Seminole, and Osage; provisions still in force of the treaties with the United States of 1790, 1803, 1826, 1832, 1834, 1839, and 1856; and the treaty of 1866.

251 copies are known, from Creek tribal records, to have been printed. The constitution appears here rewritten and rearranged for greater clearness but there are no changes in its provisions.

*Revised statutes, in Creek.* 1882.

Este-Maskoke em ahaka, momet ahaka-em-pataka. L. C. Perryman etoh tal hoecate. Fotskat talofan eshotop hoyatet os; ohrolop 1881 omof. [Fort Scott, Kansas, 1882.] [172

94 p. 22 cm.

The contents of the preceding volume, translated into Creek by Legus Chouteau Perryman (1838–1922).

The volume was printed by John H. Rice & Sons at the office of the *Fort Scott Monitor.* 300 copies are known, from Creek tribal records, to have been printed.

Fotskat in the title is the Creek rendition of Fort Scott.

OkHi OkTG

Enactments of the National Council of the Muskogee Nation, during the sessions of 1880 and 1881. Levison & Blythe Stationery Co. print, St. Louis. [1882.] [173

20 p. 23 cm. Printed wrappers.

The acts and resolutions of the regular October sessions of 1880 and 1881, and two decisions of the Creek supreme court delivered October 22, 1881.

200 copies are known, from Creek tribal records, to have been printed.

DJ DLC IaU-L MnU-L OkTG

*Acts of* 1880 *and* 1881, *in Creek.* 1882.

Maskoke etvlwv, tvlwv-vlke en nvkftetv, oh-rolope 1880, momet 1881 omof vhakv hayvte. [St. Louis, 1882.] [174

21 p. 22 cm.

The contents of the preceding volume, translated into Creek by D. M. Hodge.

The volume was printed by the Levison & Blythe Stationery Company. 200 copies are known, from Creek tribal records, to have been printed.

David McKillop Hodge, a quarter blood Creek long prominent in tribal affairs, was joint compiler, with the missionary Robert McGill Loughridge, of a Creek dictionary printed at St. Louis in 1890. He served as interpreter for Chitto Harjo (Crazy Snake) when the latter made his historic appearance in 1906 before the United States Senate committee holding a hearing on Indian affairs at the old Elks' Hall at Tulsa. On that occasion Hodge said, "I have been at this work [interpreting and translating] a long time, for I commenced at twelve years of age and I am now an old man."

MH-L

Enactments of the National Council of the Muskogee Nation, during the sessions of 1880, 1881 and 1882. Levison & Blythe Stationery Co. print, St. Louis. [1883.] [175

34 p. 23 cm. Printed wrappers.

The reprinted contents of No. 173 of this bibliography, and the acts and resolutions of the regular session of October 1882.

ICLaw MnU-L OkTG

Enactments of the National Council of the Muskogee Nation, during the sessions of 1880, 1881, 1882, 1883, 1884. Muskogee, I. T.: Indian Journal Steam print, 1884. [176

44 p. 21.5 cm. Printed wrappers.

The reprinted contents of the preceding volume, and the acts and resolutions of the regular October sessions of 1883 and 1884.

MnU-L NNB OkMu OkTG

*Acts of* 1880–84, *in Creek.* 1885.

Maskoke etvlwv tvlwv-vlke en nvkvftetv oh-rolope 1880, momet 1884 omof vhakv hayvte. Muskogee, I. T.: by the Indian Journal Steam Job Office. 1885. [177

34 p. 21.5 cm. Printed wrappers.

The contents of the preceding volume, translated into Creek.

OkTG

The treaty. [Muskogee, 1889.] [178

[4] p. 25.5 cm. Caption title. Text in English and in Creek. The first two pages are printed in double columns.

The following imprint crosses the foot of pages [2] and [3] in a single line: Press of the Muskogee Phoenix, 1889.

An act of the national council, approved by the principal chief January 31, 1889, ratifying the agreement, or treaty, of January 16, 1889, by which the Creeks ceded surplus lands to the United States. The text of the agreement itself is embodied in the act.

According to a manuscript note on the Newberry Library copy, the translation into Creek was made by the Reverend H. M. Harjo.

Henry Marsey Harjo, a full blood Creek, was long a laborer in the Baptist vineyard. He served at one time as superintendent of Wealaka Mission, a Creek tribal school. The Harjo family is one of the oldest and largest in the tribe.

ICN NN

Constitution and laws of the Muskogee Nation, as compiled by L. C. Perryman, March 1st, 1890. Muskogee, Indian Ter.: Phoenix Printing Company, 1890. [179

250 p. 21.5 cm.

The constitution, the civil and criminal code of 1867 with amendments, and compiled statutes with amendments; collected acts and resolutions of the regular October sessions annually from 1880 to 1889, inclusive, and the extra sessions of January and June 1889; two Creek supreme court decisions of 1881; United States statutes affecting Creek citizens; the compact of June 1870 with the Cherokee, Seminole, and Osage, and the amended compact of June 1887; provisions still in force of the treaties with the United States of 1790, 1803, 1826, 1832, 1834, 1839, and 1856; and the treaty of 1866.

Legus Chouteau Perryman (1838–1922), the compiler, was at the time principal chief.

Creek cattle law. An act establishing quarantine regulations against foreign cattle and to prevent smuggling cattle into the Creek Nation. [Muskogee? 1890.] [180

[3] p. 20.5 cm. Caption title.

The act was passed October 29, 1890.

OkHi

Rules of the House of Warriors, compiled and translated by A. P. McKellop, Clerk of the House of Warriors. 1892. Muskogee, Ind. Ter., Phoenix Printing Company. [181

11 p. 14.5 cm. Printed wrappers. Text in English and in Creek.

Albert Pike McKellop (b. 1858) was at various times council member, district judge, attorney general, and national delegate. He had three-fourths Creek blood.

OkTG

Constitution and laws of the Muskogee Nation, as compiled and codified by A. P. McKellop, under act of October 15, 1892. Muskogee, Indian Ter.: F. C. Hubbard, printer. 1893. [182

243 p. 22 cm.

United States patent of August 11, 1852, to Creek lands; the constitution, and revised statutes; the compact of June 1870 with the Cherokee, Seminole, and Osage, and the amended compact of June 1887; United States statutes affecting Creek citizens; provisions still in force of the treaties with the United States of 1790, 1803, 1826, 1832, 1834, 1839, and 1856; the treaty of 1866; and forms for use in civil and criminal cases.

1000 copies were ordered printed.

Frank Clarence Hubbard (1864–1930) was a native of Indiana who learned the printer's craft at Carthage, Missouri. He was long an editor and banker at Muskogee and was once elected mayor of the town.

*Revised statutes, in Creek.* 1894.

Este Maskoke etvlwv emvhakv empvtakv momet emvhakv. D. C. Watson, etohtvlhocvtet os ot'voskv rvkko ennetta 15, 1892, vhakv hakvte vcvkvyen. Maskoke estecate etvlwv: E. H. Hubbard & Co., svnoricvlke, 1894. [Muskogee, 1894.] [183

[1], 192, xxvii, [1] p. 21.5 cm.

The contents of the preceding volume, translated into Creek. The forms for use in civil and criminal cases are omitted.

Daniel C. Watson, the translator, was a native Creek who served at one time as the secretary of Principal Chief Ward Coachman.

Ernest Henry Hubbard (1871– ), a half-brother of Frank C. Hubbard, ran their jointly owned printing business while the latter served for a time as postmaster at Muskogee. Like his brother, Mr. Hubbard learned the printer's craft at Carthage, Missouri. He lives (1946) at Muskogee.

Acts and resolutions of the National Council of the Muskogee Nation of 1893. Compiled by W. A. Rentie. Muskogee, Ind. Ter., The Phoenix Printing Company. 1894. [184

[2], ii, 21, [2], 28 p. 21.5 cm. Printed wrappers. Text in English and in Creek.

Variant: The Library of Congress copy has the following erroneous paging in the Creek version: 17/22, 23/20, 21/18, 19/[24(blank)]. The text is regular and uninterrupted.

The acts and resolutions of the regular session of October 1893, an act of 1891 which became a law by limitation, and two Creek supreme court decisions of 1881 and two of 1883.

1000 copies were ordered printed.

W. A. Rentie, the compiler, was a negro member of the Creek tribe and a lawyer who practised in the tribal courts. He was born, in 1862, a slave of Roley McIntosh, the well-known Creek Indian. Rentie was once elected to the house of warriors, the lower branch of the council, a distinction possibly reflected in his registration on the final roll of Creek freedmen as Warrior Rentie.

DJ DLC MH-L MiU-L MnU-L NNB OkMu OkTG

The new constitution of the Muskogee Nation. Proposed under act of the National Council, approved, November 2, 1893. English and Indian. Indian Journal Printing Company, printers, Eufaula, I. T. 1894. [185

25 p. 22 cm. Printed wrappers.

The proposed constitution, which was drafted by a committee of which Napoleon Bonaparte Childers (b. 1844) was the chairman and George Washington Grayson (1843–1920) the secretary, was rejected at a general election in June 1894.

Angie Debo, *The Road to Disappearance* (1941), 353: "The Indians favored it by a substantial majority, but it was defeated by the almost unanimous vote of the negroes, who would have lost their influence in the Council by the [proposed] change in representation."

**ICN MH-L MnU-L NN OkTG**

Acts and resolutions of the Creek National Council of the extra session of April, 1894, and the regular session of October, 1894. Compiled and translated by D. C. Watson. Muskogee, Ind. Ter.: E. H. Hubbard & Co., printers. 1894. [186

19, [1], 22, [1] p. 22 cm. Printed wrappers. Text in English and in Creek.

The contents are fully described in the title.

Acts and resolutions of the Creek National Council of the extra session of January, 1895. Compiled and translated by D. C. Watson. Muskogee, Ind. Ter.: E. H. Hubbard & Co., printers. 1895. [187

12, 12 p. 22 cm. Printed wrappers. Text in English and in Creek.

The contents are fully described in the title.

**DJ DLC ICLaw In-SC M MH-L MnU-L NNB OkTG**

Acts and resolutions of the Creek National Council of the sessions of May, June, October, November and December, 1895. Compiled and translated by D. C. Watson. Muskogee: The Phoenix Printing Co., 1896. [188

40 p. 21 cm. Printed wrappers. Text in English and in Creek.

The contents are fully described in the title.

**DJ In-SC NNLI OkTG PPB**

Acts and resolutions of the Creek National Council of the called session of August, and the regular session of October, 1896. With Creek translation. Compiled and translated by D. C. Watson. Muskogee, Ind. Ter.: The Phoenix Printing Company. MDCCCXCVI. [189

23, 25 p. 22 cm. Printed wrappers.

The contents are fully described in the title.

**DJ M MH-L OkTG**

Acts and resolutions of the National Council of the Muskogee Nation of 1893 and 1899, inclusive. Muskogee, Ind. Ter.: Phoenix Printing Company, 1900. [190

94, iv p. 23 cm. Issued in a printed wrapper and also in a cloth binding.

"All the acts and resolutions of the council from 1893 to 1899, inclusive."

500 copies were printed.

The Creek mixed blood Albert Pike McKellop (b. 1858) was the compiler.

**DLC ICN IaU-L MH-L MiU-L MnU-L Ok OkHi OkTG**

Permit law of the Muskogee Nation, approved November 5, 1900. [Okmulgee? 1900.] [191

4 p. 21.5 cm.

**MnU-L OkHi OkTG**

Rules of the House of Warriors adopted December 7, 1903. Okmulgee, Ind. Ter. Chieftain Printing House. [1903.] [192

15 p. 15 cm. Printed wrappers. Text in English and in Creek.

**DLC OkHi OkTG OkU-P**

Ordinances of the City of Muskogee. [Muskogee, 1904.] [193

[2], 99 p. 22.5 cm. Wrapper title.

Ordinances passed by the council from July 5, 1898, to February 12, 1904, inclusive.

**DLC**

**Message of Moty Tiger, Principal Chief of the Creek Nation, to the extra-ordinary session of the National Council of said Nation called by authority of an act of Congress, which convened at Okmulgee on September 1st, 1914, and the actions and proceedings thereof in the Creek and English languages. Rendered into Creek by G. W. Grayson. [Eufaula, 1914.]** [194

[1], 64 p. 22.5 cm. Wrapper title.

The following imprint appears on the back wrapper: Indian Journal, printers, Eufaula, Oklahoma.

Message of Principal Chief Moty Tiger (1834?–1921), resolutions, council rules, and committee reports.

This final session of the quiescent Creek council was held for the discharge of long unfinished tribal business. Special authority to revive the council for the purpose was granted by Congress to the principal chief in a clause of the Indian appropriation act of 1914.

George Washington Grayson or Yahu Tustunuke[6] (1843–1920), the translator, was an influential Creek quarter blood of Scottish descent. Educated at tribal expense in Arkansas, he returned to serve his people in many positions of trust and honor. Translator of this final official publication of the Creek Nation, he also had a hand in the first, almost half a century earlier, for he served as secretary of the convention at Black Jack Grove which adopted the 1867 constitution. Mr. Grayson showed no trace of his Indian blood.

**DSI-E OkTG**

[6] That is, wolf warrior.

Wrapper Title of No. 207

ADDITIONAL LAWS

OF THE

SAC AND FOX NATION,

INDIAN TERRITORY.

PASSED AT SESSION OF OCTOBER, 1889.

VINITA, IND. TER.:
PRESS OF THE INDIAN CHIEFTAIN.
1890.

Title Page of No. 212

# THE INDIAN TERRITORY

Under a provision of the 1866 treaties looking toward eventual territorial status for the Indians, delegates from the principal tribes in Indian Territory assembled in 1870 at Okmulgee, Creek Nation, and took steps, including the adoption of a constitution, to set up a general government of their own. The constitution was never ratified by all the member tribes but the so-called Okmulgee Council continued to meet for several years, a mutually profitable gathering of leaders of the civilized tribes and of the wild tribes to the West. The council was discontinued when Congress withdrew its financial support.

Journal of the General Council of the Indian Territory, composed of delegates duly elected from the Indian tribes legally resident thereof, assembled in council at Okmulgee, in the Indian Territory, under the provisions of the twelfth article of the treaty made and concluded at the City of Washington, in the year 1866, between the United States and the Cherokee Nation, and similar treaties between the United States and the Choctaw and Chickasaw, Muskokee, and Seminole tribes of Indians, of the same date. Lawrence: Excelsior Book and Job Printing Office. 1871. [195

64 p. 20.5 cm. Printed wrappers.

Journals of the first session of September and the adjourned session of December 1870. The journals include resolutions, council rules, and committee reports. Pages [44]–57 contain the constitution of Indian Territory adopted by the council December 20, 1870.

The presiding officer of this and of all subsequent sessions of the Okmulgee Council was Enoch Hoag (1812–1884), a member of the Society of Friends who served from 1869 to 1876 as Superintendent of Indian Affairs for the Central Indian Superintendency. He made his headquarters at Lawrence, Kansas, and probably himself made the arrangements for the printing of the council journals.

The chairman of the committee which drafted the constitution was William Potter Ross (1820–1891), a former principal chief of the Cherokee Nation and one of the leading citizens of Indian Territory.

The secretary of the council was George Washington Grayson (1843–1920), a prominent Creek Indian of mixed blood.

The opening session of the Okmulgee Council marked the last public appearance of the great Stand Watie; he served as one of the Cherokee delegates but apparently took little part in the proceedings.

**DSI-E KHi MH MH-L OkTG**

**Journal of the second annual session** of the General Council of the Indian Territory, composed of delegates duly elected from the Indian tribes legally resident therein, assembled in council, at Okmulgee, Indian Territory, from the 5th to the 14th (inclusive) of June, 1871, under the provisions of the twelfth article of the treaty made and concluded at the City of Washington in the year 1866, between the United States and the Cherokee Nation, and similar treaties between the United States and the Choctaw and Chickasaw, Muscokee and Seminole tribes of Indians, of same date. Lawrence, Kansas: Journal Book and Job Printing House. 1871. [196

20 p. 21 cm. Printed wrappers.

The journal includes resolutions, committee reports, and an additional schedule to the constitution.

500 copies were ordered printed.

**DLC DSI-E KHi MB NN**

**Journal of the third annual session** of the General Council of the Indian Territory, composed of delegates duly elected from the Indian tribes legally resident therein, assembled in council, at Okmulgee, Indian Territory, from the 3d to the 18th (inclusive) of June, 1872, under the provisions of the twelfth article of the treaty made and concluded at the City of Washington in the year 1866, between the United States and the Cherokee Nation, and similar treaties between the United States and the Choctaw and Chickasaw, Muscokee and Seminole tribes of Indians, of same date. Lawrence, Kansas: Journal Book and Job Printing House. 1872. [197

34 p. 21 cm. Printed wrappers.

The journal includes resolutions, council rules, and committee reports.

500 copies were ordered printed.

DLC DNA DSI-E KHi OkTG

Journal of the fourth annual session of the General Council of the Indian Territory, composed of delegates duly elected from the Indian tribes legally resident therein, assembled in council at Okmulgee, Indian Territory, from the 5th to the 15th (inclusive) of May, 1873, under the provisions of the twelfth article of the treaty made and concluded at the City of Washington in the year 1866, between the United States and the Cherokee Nation, and similar treaties between the United States and the Choctaw and Chickasaw, Muscokee and Seminole tribes of Indians, of same date. Lawrence, Kansas: Journal Steam Book and Job Printing House. 1873. [198

38 p. 20 cm. Printed wrappers.

The journal includes resolutions and committee reports.

1500 copies were ordered printed.

DLC DSI-E KHi OkTG TxU

Journal of the fourth annual session of the General Council of the Indian Territory, composed of delegates duly elected from the Indian tribes legally resident therein, assembled in council, at Okmulgee, Indian Territory, Dec. 1st, 1873, under the provisions of the twelfth article of the treaty made and concluded at the City of Washington in the year 1866, between the United States and the Cherokee Nation and similar treaties between the United States and Choctaw and Chickasaw, Muscokee and Seminole tribes of Indians, of same date. [Boggy Depot? 1874.] [199

34 p. 22.5 cm. Printed wrappers.

This was an adjourned session. The journal includes resolutions and committee reports.

1000 copies were ordered printed.

Not a very finished production, the volume was obviously not executed by the printers of the earlier and later journals. The place of printing is conjectured from the similarity of typography and paper to those of a pamphlet printed at Boggy Depot a short time earlier.

OkHi OkTG

Journal of the fifth annual session of the General Council of the Indian Territory, composed of delegates duly elected from the Indian tribes legally resident therein, assembled in council at Okmulgee, Indian Territory, from the 4th to the 14th (inclusive) of May, 1874, under the provisions of the twelfth article of the treaty made and concluded at the City of Washington in the year 1866, between the United States and the Cherokee Nation, and similar treaties between the United States and the Choctaw and Chickasaw, Muscogee and Seminole tribes of Indians, of same date. Lawrence, Kansas: Journal Steam Book and Job Printing House. 1874. [200

58 p. 21 cm. Printed wrappers.

The journal includes resolutions and committee reports.

1200 copies were ordered printed.

DLC DSI-E KHi OkHi OkTG TxU

Journal of the sixth annual session of the General Council of the Indian Territory, composed of delegates duly elected from the Indian tribes legally resident therein, assembled in council at Okmulgee, Indian Territory, from the 3d to the 15th (inclusive) of May, 1875, under the provisions of the twelfth article of the treaty made and concluded at the City of Washington in the year 1866, between the United States and the Cherokee Nation, and similar treaties between the United States and the Choctaw and Chickasaw, Muscogee and Seminole tribes of Indians, of same date. Lawrence, Kansas: Republican Journal Steam Printing Establishment. 1875.

114 p. 21 cm. Printed wrappers. [201

The journal includes resolutions, council rules, and committee reports. Pages [99]–114 contain the amended constitution.

1200 copies were ordered printed.

CSmH DLC DNA DSI-E M MH-L MnHi NN OkTG TxU

Journal of the adjourned session of the sixth annual General Council of the Indian Territory, composed of delegates duly elected from the Indian tribes legally resident therein, assembled in council at Okmulgee, Indian Territory, from the 1st to the 9th (inclusive) of Sept., 1875, under the provisions of the twelfth article of the treaty made and concluded at the City of Washington in the year 1866, between the United States and the Cherokee Nation, and similar treaties between the United States and the Choctaw and Chickasaw, Muscogee and Seminole tribes of Indians, of same date. Lawrence, Kansas: Journal Steam Book and Job Printing House. 1875. [202

35 p. 21 cm. Printed wrappers.

The journal includes resolutions, council rules, and committee reports. Pages 8–20 contain the amended constitution.

DSI-E KHi OkHi OkTG TxU

# THE NEZ PERCÉ TRIBE

The Nez Percé Indians, a Shahaptian tribe formerly ranging over a wide territory in Idaho, Washington, and Oregon, were first observed in 1805 by Lewis and Clark. Subdued in an uprising in 1877, they were placed on several reservations, the largest of which is the Lapwai Reservation in Idaho. The laws in the following volume were supposed to be administered by chiefs.

*Code, in Nez Percé.* 1842.

Wilupupki 1842, Lapwai hipaina Takta Hwait tamalwiawat himakespinih, suiapu-miohat-upkinih. [Lapwai Mission, 1842.]

8 p. 14.5 cm. Text in Nez Percé, in the Roman alphabet. [203

The title above is the first paragraph of the text; there is no title-page or caption title. Page [1] is headed by a cut showing a spread eagle.

Introductory matter and Biblical names occupy the first three pages. The remainder of the volume is devoted to a short code of laws drafted by Elijah White (1806–1879), the United States sub-agent for Indians west of the Rocky Mountains, and the Takta Hwait of the title above, and orally and perhaps uncomprehendingly adopted, at his instance, by the chiefs of the Lapwai band of Nez Percé Indians at Lapwai, on the Clear Water River, 12 miles east of the present Lewiston, Idaho, about December 7, 1842. The same code was orally adopted later that month, between the 25th and the 29th, again at the sub-agent's instance, by the Wasco, a small Chinookan tribe living on the south side of the Columbia River, in the neighborhood of The Dalles, in the present Wasco County, Oregon. Still later, in April 1843, Doctor White secured its oral adoption by the Cayuse, a small Waiilatpuan tribe, at Waiilatpu, now Whitman, on the Walla Walla River in southeastern Washington.

The volume was printed in December 1842 on the Congregational mission press at Lapwai, the first printing press in the Northwest, by the Reverend Henry Harmon Spalding (1804–1874), a missionary sent out by the American Board of Commissioners for Foreign Missions. The translation into Nez Percé was made by Spalding, who was the first to adopt the language to Roman letters.

The American Board copy, here described, was transmitted by Spalding himself to mission headquarters at Boston; it lies bound in a manuscript volume (248) of correspondence about the Oregon Indians. The old records of the American Board are permanently deposited in the Harvard College Library. There is said to be another copy of the pamphlet in private hands in the West.

The English version of the Nez Percé laws first appeared in the annual report of the Commissioner of Indian Affairs for 1844. It will be found also in Elijah White, *A Concise View of Oregon Territory, its Colonial and Indian Relations* (Washington: T. Barnard, 1846), and in the little known *Testimonials and Records, together with Arguments in favor of Special Action for our Indian Tribes: by Dr. E. White, of San Francisco* (Washington: R. A. Waters, 1861), of which Graff has a copy.

**MH**

# THE OMAHA TRIBE

The Omaha Indians, a Siouan tribe in Nebraska since the earliest times, have lived on a reservation near the present city of Omaha since 1855. Their laws were administered by chiefs.

Code of laws, as adopted by the Chiefs and members of the Omaha Tribe of Indians, in council assembled, the 11th day of May A. D. 1860. [Omaha, 1860.] [204

4 p. 13.5 cm. Caption title.

A civil and criminal code adopted at the Omaha Reservation.

OkTG

# THE OSAGE NATION

The Osage Indians, a Siouan tribe, were first noted by Jacques Marquette as residing on the Osage River in present Missouri in 1673. By the nineteenth century they claimed and roamed over most of Missouri and southern Kansas and the northern portions of Arkansas and Oklahoma. Successive treaties reduced their holdings and in 1829 they were gathered on a reservation in southern Kansas whence they were removed in 1870 to Indian Territory.

The Osage constitution of 1861 vested legislative and judicial authority in a council which met twice a year and whose members were elected by the people and executive authority in a governor similarly chosen. Under the constitution of 1881 legislative authority was exercised by a council which met annually and whose members were elected by the people, executive authority by a principal chief similarly chosen, and judicial authority by a supreme court whose members were elected by the council.

Osage constitution. [Lawrence, Kansas, 1861.] [205

Broadside. 35 cm. 2 columns.

The following imprint appears at the end: Republican print. Lawrence.

The constitution was adopted August 31, 1861, by a convention of the Osage people "assembled at Council Village, on the north side of the Neosho River, in the Osage Nation." Joseph Swiss was president of the convention.

DNA

The constitution and laws of the Osage Nation, passed at Pawhuska, Osage Nation, in the years 1881 and 1882. Washington, D. C.: R. O. Polkinhorn, printer, 1883. [206

29 p. 23.5 cm. Wrapper title.

Constitution adopted in convention at Pawhuska, the Osage capital, December 31, 1881, and statutes adopted March 4, 1882.

The president of the convention was the half blood James Bigheart or Poñkawadaïñga,[1] who was later elected principal chief.

DLC DNA ICN MH-L NNB OkTG

**Laws of the Osage Nation**, passed at Pawhuska, Osage Nation, in the years 1883, 1884, and 1885. Muskogee, I. T.: by the Indian Journal Steam Job Office. 1885. [207

12 p. 22 cm. Printed wrappers.

Acts and resolutions of the sessions of April and November 1883, January, May, and December 1884, and March and April 1885.

OkTG

**Treaties and laws of the Osage Nation**, as passed to November 26, 1890. Compiled by W. S. Fitzpatrick. 1895. Press of the Cedar Vale Commercial, Cedar Vale, Kansas. [208

[1], [1], [1], [15], 103 p. 23 cm. Issued in sheep and also in printed wrappers.

An unconsidered blank leaf appears between p. 50 and p. 51 and thereafter every two leaves of text are followed by an unconsidered blank leaf. The running-title, United States Treaties, was not changed at the proper place and it appears throughout the volume.

Constitution and revised statutes; treaties with the United States of 1810, 1815, 1819, 1823, 1825, 1826, 1839, 1867, and 1868, and provisions affecting the Osage of the treaty of 1866 between the United States and the Cherokee; and a deed, dated June 14, 1883, from the Cherokee Nation to the Osage Nation for a portion of the Cherokee country.

William Samuel Fitzpatrick (1866–1945), the compiler, practised law as a young man in southern Kansas and in Oklahoma and Indian territories and he was for several years a member of the Kansas state senate. He later had a successful career in the oil business. Fitzpatrick was a native of Illinois.

[1] That is, playful Ponca.

# THE OTTAWA TRIBE

The Ottawa Indians, an Algonquian tribe, were first observed in Canada in 1615 by Samuel de Champlain; they later lived in scattered bands chiefly in the Great Lakes region of the United States. Those here concerned settled in eastern Kansas about 1836 and were removed in 1867 to a reservation in Indian Territory.

According to the Reverend Jotham Meeker, laws were first reduced to writing by the Ottawa about 1840. They were enacted and administered by a council composed of lawmen elected by the people.

Ottawa first book. Containing lessons for the learner; portions of the Gospel by Luke, omitted by Matthew and John; and the Ottawa laws. By Jotham Meeker, missionary of the Amer. Bap. Mis. Union. Second edition. Ottawa Baptist Mission Station. J. Meeker, printer, 1850. [209

128 p. 12.5 cm.

Revised laws, and additional laws passed January 1850, in English and Ottawa, United States whiskey laws, in Ottawa, gospel portions, and primer miscellanea.

500 copies were printed. Jotham Meeker (1804–1855), the printer, made the translation from Ottawa into English.

The first edition implied in the title was printed at the Shawanoe Mission press in 1838. It contains only the primer miscellanea and the gospel portions.

The Ottawa Baptist Mission Station was located at the present Ottawa, Kansas.

**KHi MBAt NN**

# THE SAC AND FOX NATION

The Sauk[1] and Fox tribe was born of the union in the eighteenth century of the Sauk and the Foxes, two closely related Algonquian tribes then living in Wisconsin. By the nineteenth century the united tribes had gained a large territory in Wisconsin, Iowa, and Missouri, much of which they gradually signed away in a series of treaties with the United States. Defeated in the so-called Black Hawk War in 1832, they were further stripped of lands and in 1837 were removed to Kansas. There internal dissensions arose and in 1859 the Foxes withdrew to Iowa. In 1867 the Sauk removed from Kansas to Indian Territory and later organized themselves into the Sac and Fox Nation.

The constitution of the Sac and Fox Nation vested legislative authority in a council of treaty chiefs and councillors, both elected by the people, which met annually, executive authority in a principle chief elected by the council from the treaty chiefs of its own number, and judicial authority in a supreme court whose members were elected by the council.

Constitution and laws of the Sac and Fox Nation. Indian Territory. The constitution of the Sac and Fox Nation prepared by the authorized committee and adopted by the National Council. National Free Press, No. 1108 E Street, Northwest, Washington, D. C. 1887. [210

30 p. 23 cm. Wrapper title.

Constitution adopted in convention at the Sac and Fox Agency March 26, 1885, and journal of the convention; statutes approved by the principal chief April 6, 1885, and two letters on tribal affairs.

The presiding officer of the convention was Ukquahoko[2] or Grey Eyes,

[1] Sauk is the spelling preferred by ethnologists; Sac is the official and popular spelling.
[2] That is, fish floating to the shore.

who, at his death in 1886, had been for 17 years principal chief of his tribe.

The Sac and Fox Agency lay about six miles south of the present Stroud, Oklahoma.

DIA OkTG WHi

Constitution and laws of the Sac and Fox Nation, Indian Territory. The constitution of the Sac and Fox Nation, prepared by the authorized committee, and adopted by the National Council. St. Louis and New York. Press of the August Gast Bank Note & Litho. Co. 1888. [211

30 p. 22 cm. Wrapper title.

The contents of the preceding volume and 15 amendatory acts approved by the principal chief October 27 and 28, 1887.

MH-L

Additional laws of the Sac and Fox Nation, Indian Territory. Passed at session of October, 1889. Vinita, Ind. Ter.: Press of the Indian Chieftain. 1890. [212

8 p. 22 cm. Printed wrappers.

Eleven acts.

OkHi

# THE SEMINOLE NATION

The Seminole Indians, a Muskhogean tribe formerly living in Florida, were originally emigrants from the Lower Creek towns in Georgia and Alabama. In a clash with the United States, which lasted from 1835 to 1842 and which was really a phase of the larger Creek War, the Seminole were overpowered with great cost and trouble and transported with their negroes to Indian Territory where they were at first settled against their wishes among their Creek cousins. Obtaining lands of their own in 1856, they organized themselves into the Seminole Nation and later became one, to be sure the most primitive, of the so-called Five Civilized Tribes. When the main body of the tribe was dragged off to the West a few hundred of the Seminole escaped to the Everglades in southern Florida where their descendants, a simple and reserved people, have continued to live, their persons nowadays exhibited like freaks at vacation resort side-shows and an occasional commonplace swamp killing transformed by newspaper hocus-pocus into the dark and fearful operation of ancient and immutable tribal laws of retributive justice. The most famous leader of the tribe was Osceola (1803?–1838), the son of an English trader and a Creek woman.

The earliest known written law of the Seminole is "a supplementary decree passed at the Seminole Council at the Seminole Agency,[1] Florida," November 30, 1825, "abolishing the law heretofore existing in the Nation which excludes children from the benefit of property of which the father may die possessed, and transfer[s] it to more distant relatives." The original, doubtless the work of a white hand since the Seminole were at the time almost universally unlettered, is not known to survive but the bib-

[1] The Seminole Agency was located in 1825 at Camp (later Fort) King, the germ of the present Ocala, Florida.

liographer owns in the Hitchcock papers an unpublished manuscript copy made in 1856 from Seminole tribal records, in English, in the office of the Creek Agency in Indian Territory.

Authority, such as it was, in the Seminole tribe before removal was exercised by a head chief and a council of district and town chiefs. After organization of the government in the West executive authority was exercised by a principal chief and legislative and judicial authority by a council of clan chiefs.

An act to provide for the appointment of Townsite Commissioners and the location of a town in the Seminole Nation. [Holdenville? 1897.] [213

[4] p. 22 cm. Caption title.

The act was passed by the general council April 23, 1897, at the village of Wewoka, by one provision of the act designated the capital of the Seminole Nation. The council had formerly held its meetings at the campground and springs about a mile away where, until 1890, a brush-covered arbor served as the tribal capitol.

The place of printing is conjectured from the circumstance that the *Holdenville Times* had at this date the printing press closest to Wewoka.

The Seminole in Indian Territory adopted a written constitution shortly after their separation in 1856 from the Creeks but its text has not been found. The office of the Superintendent of the Five Civilized Tribes Agency at Muskogee, Oklahoma, has in its files an unpublished manuscript volume containing some acts passed by the council in the years 1884, 1886, 1887, and 1893.[2] Three of the later acts appear in English; all the others are in Seminole, a dialect of the parent Creek language. The record book was kept by John Frippo Brown (1843–1919), the mixed blood principal chief, by whom the acts passed in 1886 and afterward were approved. The same office has also an unpublished typewritten translation into English of the acts passed by the council from 1897 to 1903. The translation, from Seminole originals in private hands, was made in 1906 by George Washington Grayson (1843–1920), a prominent Creek Indian.

**DNA**

[2] I am indebted to Mrs. Rella W. Looney, of the Oklahoma Historical Society, for directing me to this volume.

# THE SENECA NATION

The Seneca Indians, an Iroquoian tribe, have lived since earliest times in western New York, where those comprising the Seneca Nation are now scattered on three reservations. Smaller groups live in Canada and Oklahoma.

Organized government with written laws apparently began with a constitution adopted July 29, 1833, by "the Chiefs and Headmen convened at the Council House at Buffalo Creek Reservation." An unpublished contemporary manuscript copy, certified by tribal officials, is preserved in the National Archives.

Under the constitution of 1833 legislative and executive authority was exercised by chiefs and headmen or warriors. The constitution of 1848 and all later constitutions vested legislative authority in a council, executive authority in a president, and judicial authority in boards of peacemakers. All officers were elected by the people.

Declaration of the Seneca Nation of Indians in General Council assembled, with the accompanying documents, also an address to the Chiefs and people, of that Nation. Baltimore: printed by Wm. Wooddy, corner of Market and Calvert sts. 1845. [214

53 p. 21 cm. Printed wrappers.

The declaration, or ordinance, is an amendment of the 1833 constitution. Adopted January 30, 1845, "by the chiefs and representatives in general council of the whole nation" at Cattaraugus Reservation, it imposed constitutional restrictions on the alienation of tribal lands.

The presiding officer of the convention was John Seneca, one of the chiefs.

The Hicksite Friends in Baltimore, long active in missionary work among the Seneca, published this and several other volumes for their benefit.

DLC MBAt MWA OkTG PHi

*Acts of 1847, in Seneca.* 1847.

Ho di'ah heh'oh ga as'hah geh oi wah geh odoh oh jut hoh 4, 1847. [Cattaraugus Reservation, 1847.] [215

Broadside. Text in Seneca.

No copy of the original is known. The *Mental Elevator* (Cattaraugus Reservation), I (1848), 122–125, contains five council acts preceded by this editorial note: The following Resolutions were originally printed as a hand-bill, and the type having been left standing, they are inserted here simply for their preservation as a specimen of the language involving principles not destitute of value to the learner; and the English is appended to facilitate his investigations.

The English version has the following caption: Resolutions of Council, passed December 4, 1847.

The translation into Seneca was probably the work of the missionary Asher Wright (1803–1875).

A few other acts and resolutions of the Seneca council will be found in the *Mental Elevator,* an irregular little missionary periodical of which the Gilcrease Foundation has a file containing seventeen of the nineteen numbers issued.

Constitution of the Seneca Nation of Indians. Baltimore; printed by William Wooddy & Son. 1848. [216

15 p. 21 cm.

Constitution and resolutions adopted in convention at the Cattaraugus Reservation December 4, 1848, and appointment as "ambassador" to Washington of Philip E. Thomas, of Baltimore, a prominent member of the Hicksite Friends.

The president of the convention was Solomon McLane. Before its adjournment the convention appointed McLane superintendent of schools for the Allegany Reservation.

DLC CSmH MH-L NN OkTG PHi WHi

*Civil code, in Seneca.* 1854.

Neh noya'nes ha'wahdenyoh. Oi'wah geh odoh oh nisah' 28, 1854. [Cattaraugus Reservation, 1854.] [217

24 p. 21 cm. Caption title. Text in Seneca and in English.

The English version has the following caption: Laws of the Seneca Nation. Passed January 28, 1854.

A civil code.

First written in English, the code was translated into Seneca by Nicholson Henry Parker or Gaiewahgowa[1] (1822–1892), a prominent member of the tribe.

**DSI-E**

Constitution of the "Government by Chiefs," of the Seneca Nation of Indians. Adopted Nov. 30, 1854, by the National Council, subject to the approval of the electors of the Nation. Buffalo: Steam Press of Thomas & Lathrops, Commercial Advertiser Building. 1854. [218

8 p. 22.5 cm.

The text of a constitution adopted March 18, 1862, at the council house on the Cattaraugus Reservation will be found in the annual report of the Commissioner of Indian Affairs for 1892.

**MiU-L N-L**

Amended constitution of the Seneca Nation of Indians, adopted January 13th, 1893. Printed by order of the Council. Salamanca, N. Y.: Cattaraugus Republican Printing House. 1893. [219

6 p. 22.5 cm. Wrapper title.

The revised constitution adopted in conventions "at the Council House at Coldspring, on the Allegany Reservation; and also at the Court House on the Cattaraugus Reservation."

The chairman of the committee of three which revised the constitution was Wallace Halftown.

**OkTG**

Amended constitution of the Seneca Nation of Indians of 1898. [Salamanca? 1898.] [220

[7] p. on 1 leaf, broadsheet, folded accordionwise. 15.2 cm.

The constitution was adopted in conventions November 15 "at the

[1] That is, great or mighty message. Gaiewahgowa was one of the hereditary names of the Wolf clan of the Seneca. I am here indebted to Parker's grandson, Dr. Arthur C. Parker, of Rochester, New York.

Council House at Cold Spring on the Allegany Reservation; and also at the Court House on the Cattaraugus Reservation."

The presiding officers of the two conventions were William C. Hoag and Alfred Jimeson.

DIA-S

# THE STATE OF SEQUOYAH

The attempt of the principal tribes in Indian Territory in 1905 to gain admission into the Union as the State of Sequoyah was their last great effort, like all the others foredoomed to failure, to arrest the now rapid decay of tribal autonomy and to avoid inclusion in the proposed State of Oklahoma.

Constitution of the State of Sequoyah. [Muskogee, 1905.] [221

68 p. 25.5 cm. Caption title. Folded color map.

The official printing of the constitution of the proposed Indian state, which was adopted September 8, 1905, at Muskogee, Creek Nation, by a convention of the people of Indian Territory and ratified November 7 at a general election.

The map, lithographed by the August Gast Bank Note and Lithograph Company, of St. Louis, shows proposed county divisions.

The volume was printed at the *Phoenix* office.

The president of the Sequoyah convention was Pleasant Porter (1840–1907), the mixed blood principal chief of the Creek Nation, a large ranch operator, and long one of the foremost citizens of Indian Territory. The secretary of the convention was Alexander Lawrence Posey (1873–1908), the mixed blood Creek poet.

OkTG

Constitution of the State of Sequoyah. [Muskogee, 1905.] [222

A later printing, identical with the preceding volume except that the numbering of p. 68 has been dropped and the following imprint added at the foot of that page: Phoenix Printing Co., Muskogee, I. T.

CSmH DLC KHi MH-L NN OkHi OkTG Graff Streeter

Complete text of the proposed Sequoyah constitution. For sale by State Capital Company, Guthrie, Oklahoma. Price 25 cents. [Guthrie, 1905.] [223

[50] p. 21.5 cm. Printed wrappers.

An unofficial printing.

OkHi

# THE STOCKBRIDGE AND MUNSEE TRIBE

The Stockbridge Indians, a tribe of the Mohican confederacy, removed in 1785 from western Massachusetts to New York and thence in 1833 to Wisconsin.

Organized government with written laws was apparently inaugurated by the tribe on February 7, 1837, when a constitution was adopted "by the Chiefs and Warriors of the Stockbridge Nation in General Council held at the Stockbridge School house." There is an unpublished contemporary manuscript copy in the National Archives.

All functions of the Stockbridge government were exercised by a council which met twice a year and whose members were elected by the people. The member receiving the greatest number of votes succeeded to the office of supreme first magistrate, or sachem, and held executive authority. The sachem and the two council members receiving the second and third highest numbers of votes exercised judicial authority.

The Munsee, a small division of the Delawares living in New York, joined the Stockbridges in their removal in 1833 to Wisconsin. The two tribes were united in 1857 and have since been officially regarded as one.

The Stockbridge and Munsee constitution borrowed the main features of the Stockbridge constitution of 1837.

Articles of union and confederation made and adopted by the Chiefs, braves and warriors of the Stockbridge and Munsee Tribe, January 6th, 1857. Ryan & Bro., printers, Appleton, Wisconsin. [1871.] [224

8 p. 15.5 cm. Wrapper title.

The constitution of the united tribes, adopted in council at the "new fire-place, at Muh-he-con-neeh," the Stockbridge and Munsee reservation, in the present Shawano County, Wisconsin. The presiding officer was Ziba T. Peters, the sachem. The council met at the house of Aaron Konkapot, the tribal sheriff.

There is internal evidence that the volume was printed in 1871.

WHi

# THE WINNEBAGO TRIBE

The Winnebago Indians, a Siouan tribe, were first observed in Wisconsin in 1634 by Jean Nicolet. Gradually stripped of their lands by the whites, they removed from place to place until 1866 when they were given a reservation on lands of the Omaha tribe in northeastern Nebraska. Their laws were administered by chiefs.

**Laws and regulations adopted by the Winnebago Tribe of Indians, in council held at the Winnebago Agency, Nebraska, July 21st, A. D. 1868. Omaha: Daily Herald Book and Job Printing Establishment. 1868.** [225

6 p. 21 cm. Printed wrappers.

A civil and criminal code.

These laws have wholly passed from the memory of the tribe, old and well-informed Winnebago men having never heard of them.

Some time in 1856, while they were living on a reservation in Minnesota, the Winnebago adopted a written code of laws whose text has not been found.

**MnHi OkTG**

# APPENDIX

## THOMAS JEFFERSON TO THE CHEROKEE DEPUTIES

My Children, Deputies of the Cherokee Upper Towns.

I have maturely considered the speeches you have delivered me, and will now give you answers to the several matters they contain.

You inform me of your anxious desires to engage in the industrious pursuits of agriculture and civilized life; that finding it impracticable to induce the nation at large to join in this, you wish a line of separation to be established between the Upper and Lower Towns, so as to include all the waters of the Highwassee in your part; and that having thus contracted your society within narrower limits, you propose, within these, to begin the establishment of fixed laws and of regular government. You say, that the Lower Towns are satisfied with the divisions you propose, and on these several matters you ask my advice and aid.

With respect to the line of division between yourselves and the Lower Towns, it must rest on the joint consent of both parties. The one you propose appears moderate, reasonable and well defined; we are willing to recognize those on each side of that line as distinct societies, and if our aid shall be necessary to mark it more plainly than nature has done, you shall have it. I think with you, that on this reduced scale, it will be more easy for you to introduce the regular administration of laws.

In proceeding to the establishment of laws, you wish to adopt them from ours, and such only for the present as suit your present condition; chiefly indeed, those for the punishment of crimes and the protection of property. But who is to determine which of our laws suit your condition, and shall be in force with you? All of you being equally free, no one has a right to say what shall be law for the others. Our way is to put these questions to the vote, and to consider that as law for which the majority votes—the fool has as great a right to express his opinion by vote as the wise, because he is equally free, and equally master of himself. But as it would be inconvenient for all your men to meet in one place, would it not be better for every town to do as we do—that is to say: Choose by the vote of the majority of the town and of the country people nearer to that than to any other town, one, two, three or more, according to the size of the town, of those whom each voter thinks the wisest and honestest men of their place, and let these meet together and agree which of our laws suit them. But these men know nothing of our laws. How then can they know which to adopt? Let them associate in their council our beloved man living with them, Colonel Meigs, and he will tell them what our law is on any point they desire. He will inform them also of our methods of doing business in our councils, so as to preserve order and to obtain the vote of every member fairly. This council can make a law for giving to every head of a family a separate parcel of land, which, when he has built upon and improved, it shall belong to him and his descendants forever, and which the nation itself shall have no right to sell from under his feet. They will determine too, what punishment shall be inflicted for every crime. In our States generally, we punish murder only by death, and all other crimes by solitary confinement in a prison.

But when you shall have adopted laws, who are to execute them? Perhaps it may be best to permit every town and the settlers in its neighborhood attached to it, to select some of their best men, by a majority of its voters, to be judges in all differences, and to execute the law according to their own judgment. Your council of representatives will decide on this, or such other mode as may best suit you. I suggest these things, my children, for the consideration of the Upper Towns of your nation, to be decided on as they think best, and I sincerely wish you may succeed in your laudable endeavors to save the remains of your nation, by adopting industrious occupations and a government of regular laws. In this you may rely on the counsel and assistance of the Government of the United States. Deliver these words to your people in my name, and assure them of my friendship.

THOMAS JEFFERSON

January 9, 1809.

# INDEX

[The numbers refer to pages]

INDEX

# INDEX

## INDEX

## INDEX

www.ingramcontent.com/pod-product-compliance
Lightning Source LLC
Chambersburg PA
CBHW031505180326
41458CB00060B/435
*9781584772606*